William Francis Collier

History of Rome

William Francis Collier
History of Rome
ISBN/EAN: 9783744764667
Printed in Europe, USA, Canada, Australia, Japan
Cover: Foto ©ninafisch / pixelio.de

More available books at **www.hansebooks.com**

Nelson's School Series.

HISTORY OF ROME.

BY

WILLIAM FRANCIS COLLIER, LL.D.,

TRINITY COLLEGE, DUBLIN;

Author of "School History of the British Empire," "English History for Junior Classes,"
"The Great Events of History," "History of English Literature," &c.

LONDON:
T. NELSON AND SONS, PATERNOSTER ROW;
EDINBURGH; AND NEW YORK.

MDCCCLXVII.

DR. COLLIER'S HISTORIES OF GREECE AND ROME.
(*Each to be had separately.*)

NOTE.

THESE volumes aim at giving a clear outline of the chief events in Grecian and Roman History.

The personal or biographical element, upon which so much of the living interest of History mainly depends, has been kept prominently in view throughout.

The same plan has been followed as that adopted in the author's "Great Events of History;" and among other features of similarity to that work, these volumes contain Lists, which will enable a pupil to become acquainted with the leading names in Greek and Roman Literature.

June, 1866.

CONTENTS.

FIRST PERIOD.

CHAPTER I.—THE SEVEN KINGS OF ROME.

Building of Rome—Romulus and Numa—Horatii and Curiatii—Tarquin the Elder—Elevation of the Plebs—Death of Servius—Tarquin the Proud—Story of Lucretia 1

CHAPTER II.—THE TARQUINS IN EXILE.

The New Government—Brutus and his Sons—Death of Brutus—Horatius and the Bridge—Mucius Scævola—The Swimming Girls—The First Dictator—Battle of Lake Regillus 8

CHAPTER III.—TRIBUNES OF THE PLEBS.

State of the Plebs—A Piteous Tale—The First Secession—Menenius' Story—Tribunes Appointed—Their Powers 12

CHAPTER IV.—PATRICIAN HEROES.

Coriolanus: the Fabii—Patrician Legends—Coriolanus—The Agrarian Law—Cincinnatus—The Camp at Cremera—The Valley of Algidus... 15

CHAPTER V.—THE DECEMVIRS.

The New Code—The Ten Appointed—First Year—Second Year—Story of Dentatus—Story of Virginia 18

CHAPTER VI.—CAMILLUS AND THE GAULS.

The Struggle continued—Siege of Veii—Battle of the Alia—Gauls in the Forum—Geese Save the Capitol—The Weighing of the Gold—The Torc and the Crow 22

CHAPTER VII.—THE LICINIAN ROGATIONS.

The City Rebuilt—Fate of Manlius—Licinian Rogations—Details of the Strife—Victory of the Plebs—Temple of Concord—Steps gained by Plebs 27

SECOND PERIOD.

CHAPTER I.—THE SAMNITE AND LATIN WARS.

Curtius—The Samnites—First War—Latin War—Second War—Caudine Forks—Third War—Battle of Sentinum.. 30

CHAPTER II.—THE CAMPAIGNS OF PYRRHUS.

Tarentum—Battle of Heraclea—Cineas—Battle of Asculum—Pyrrhus in Sicily—Defeated at Beneventum... 35

CHAPTER III.—THE FIRST PUNIC WAR.

Cause of the War—First Roman Fleet—Mylæ and Ecnomus—Invasion of Africa—Regulus—Siege of Lilybænm—Battle of Ægusa—Peace......... 38

CHAPTER IV.—THE SECOND OR GREAT PUNIC WAR.

Illyrian and Gallic Wars—Hannibal—Siege of Saguntum—Hannibal's March—Ticino; Trebia; Trasimene—Fabius Cunctator—Battle of Cannæ—Sieges of Syracuse and Capua—Scipio in Spain—Hasdrubal's March—The Metaurus—Scipio in Africa—Battle of Zama—Peace....... 45

CHAPTER V.—THE THIRD PUNIC WAR.

Cato the Censor—His Triumph over Scipio Major—Death of Hannibal—Delenda est Carthago—Two Useless Years—Scipio in Command—Fall of Carthage... 61

CHAPTER VI.—WARS IN SPAIN AND SICILY.

Treaty of Gracchus—Massacre of Galba—Viriathus—Celtiberian War—Numantia—Roman Slaves—Servile War in Sicily............................ 66

CHAPTER VII.—THE GRACCHI.

Tiberius Gracchus—His Agrarian Law—Slain in the Capitol—Death of Scipio Minor—Caius Gracchus—Sempronian Laws—Death of Caius—Cornelia.. 70

Great Names of Roman Literature, &c.... 76

THIRD PERIOD.

CHAPTER I.—MARIUS AND SULLA.

Jugurthine War—Teutones and Cimbri—Saturninus and Drusus—Social War—First Mithridatic War—Flight of Marius—Marius in Rome—His Death—Return of Sulla—The Colline Gate—Proscriptions—Puteoli... 77

CHAPTER II.—POMPEY AND CÆSAR.

Sertorian War—Spartacus—The Cilician Pirates—Third Mithridatic War—Catiline and Cicero—First Triumvirate—Cæsar in Gaul—The Rubicon—Pharsalia—Murder of Pompey—Thapsus and Munda—Murder of Cæsar... 89

Great Names of the First Century B.C.... 108

CHAPTER III.—MARK ANTONY.

The Funeral Speech—Battle of Mutina—Second Triumvirate—Death of Cicero—Battle of Philippi—Cleopatra's Galley—Defeat of Sextus Pompey—Sloth of Antony—Battle of Actium—Death of Antony and Cleopatra... 110

CHAPTER IV.—THE REIGN OF AUGUSTUS.

Called Augustus—His Ministers—Works of Peace—The Prætorian Guards—Wars of Augustus—The Legions of Varus—Domestic Life—Death of Augustus... 120

Great Names of the First Century A.D... 124

CHAPTER V.—THE UNWORTHY CÆSARS.

Germanicus—Sejanus—Island of Capreæ—Freaks of Caligula—Claudius Invades Britain—Caractacus—Cruelties of Nero—Boadicea—The Great Fire—A wretched Coward.. 126

CHAPTER VI.—TO THE FALL OF ROME.

Jerusalem Destroyed—Agricola in Britain—Trajan—The Antonines—Purple for Sale—Aurelian and Zenobia—Diocletian—Constantine the Great—Julian and Theodosius—Goths, Vandals, Huns—Fall of Rome 132

Later Latin Writers.. 140

ROMAN CHRONOLOGY.. 141

HISTORY OF ROME.

FIRST PERIOD.

CHAPTER I.

THE SEVEN KINGS OF ROME.

Building of Rome.	Elevation of the Plebs.
Romulus and Numa.	Death of Servius.
Horatii and Curiatii.	Tarquin the Proud.
Tarquin the Elder.	Story of Lucretia.

THE early annals of Rome, especially the story of her Seven Kings and of the events which led to the establishment of a republic, are so largely mixed with legend that it is impossible to dignify the narrative with the name of History. But it is necessary for my purpose to tell the story in its commonly accepted form.

The city of Rome grew up gradually on seven hills lying by the Tiber, about fourteen miles from its mouth. It was a favourite delusion among the Romans that they were descended from the gods; and their poets and historians dwelt lovingly on the story of Æneas the Trojan, a son of Venus, who left the ashes of his native city, and wandered long, until he found a refuge in Latium, where his son Ascanius built on the ridge of a hill a long white city (*Alba Longa*). There his descendants reigned through many generations.

A certain royal Vestal, having given birth to twin sons, of whom the god Mars was said to be the father, was buried alive; and the infants were thrown into the Tiber, then in flood. The retreating water left them stranded by a wild fig-tree, where a wolf suckled them, till a passing herdsman found them and brought them home to his wife. In his cottage the boys grew up under the names of Romulus and Remus. Restored to their position as princes, when they reached manhood, they formed the design of building a new city; but they differed in opinion as to the site. Romulus took his stand on the Palatine; Remus on the Aventine Hill, to watch the flight of birds, by which omen it was customary to decide disputes. Remus saw six vultures; and a little later Romulus saw twelve: one saw the birds sooner; the other saw a greater number. They could not agree; Remus said or did something contemptuous; and Romulus slew him on the spot.

Romulus then marked out the site of a square city on the Palatine; and this was the nucleus of ancient Rome.

It was as yet a city without people. But Romulus
753 invited all the criminals and fugitives of the sur-
B.C. rounding districts to take refuge with him; and, when the city was thus tolerably well filled with men, he got up games, to which the neighbouring citizens were invited with their wives and daughters. At the height of the festivity the young Romans seized the Sabine women and kept them in the city.

This brought on a war with the Sabines, which ended in a union of the Roman and Sabine nations, and the elevation of Titus Tatius, the Sabine chief, to an equality with Romulus in the government. The facts that Romulus took the name of *Quirinus* and the Romans that of *Quirites*, both Sabine titles, seem to show that the Sabines had to some extent the upperhand. Titus was soon killed; and after many years Romulus disappeared one day during a review in the Campus Martius—borne off in a whirlwind by his father Mars, says one legend—rent to pieces by the Sabines and carried off in bloody fragments beneath their gowns, says another and a later fiction.

Romulus is said to have organized the citizens both socially and politically. They consisted of three tribes, which were subdivided into *curiæ* and *gentes*. The Ramnes were the original Romans—the Tities were the Sabines—the Luceres appear to have been Etruscans.

After an interregnum, during which the Senate ruled, Numa Pompilius, a Sabine, was chosen King. To his gentle and pious reign were poetically ascribed the various religious institutions of the Romans, among which may be mentioned the Salii or dancing priests of Mars, who took charge of the Sacred Shields—the Pontiffs—the Flamens—Augurs—and the Vestal Virgins.

The reign of Tullus Hostilius, third King of Rome, was a time of war, chiefly with the Albans. It was during this war that the famous combat between the Horatii and the Curiatii took place, a legend embodying the historical fact that Alba was overthrown by and absorbed into Rome.

When the armies, Roman and Alban, stood face to face, it was resolved to leave the decision of the strife to the result of a triple duel to be fought between three Roman brothers called Horatii on the one hand, and three Alban brothers called Curiatii on the other. So between the lines of seated soldiers the combatants fought, until two of the Horatii lay dead; and all the Curiatii were bleeding with severe wounds. Horatius, still without a scratch, separated his opponents by pretending to run away. The least weak of the three Albans was foremost in the race of pursuit; the one whose wounds were sorest toiled along rearmost. Then, turning upon them, Horatius slew the three in succession; and, as a sign of victory, stripped them of their spoils. When he came nigh the city gate, his sister, seeing her lover's arms and dress (for she was betrothed to one of the Curiatii) carried before her exulting brother, broke into a passion of tears, which so enraged the victor that he stabbed her to death. For this he would have been hanged by a decree of the judges, had not the people interfered to save one to whose sword Rome owed so much.

When Tullus was struck dead by lightning, Ancus Martius, a Sabine, was chosen King after an interregnum. His works were rather works of peace than of war, although he subdued some of the Latin cities. He wrote the laws of Numa on a white board in the Forum—formed a rock prison in the Saturnian Hill—and built a wooden bridge over the Tiber. The foundation of Ostia, at the mouth of the river, is also ascribed to him.

The most interesting legends about Tarquinius Priscus, the fifth King of Rome, are those which narrate his elevation to the throne and the manner of his death.

He was an Etruscan stranger, born at Tarquinii, whence he removed with his wife to Rome. As he was approaching the city, an eagle came circling round his path, took off his cap, and laid it gently on his head again. This omen his wife interpreted into a sign of coming honour. His wealth and tact raised him to the favour of Ancus, who, when dying, left him guardian of his children. But Tarquin betrayed his trust, by securing his own elevation to the vacant throne.

The manner of his death was this: When the ousted sons of Ancus saw that his favourite Servius Tullius, said by some to have been the son of a female Latin slave, was likely to succeed him, they sent two peasants, who came before the King under the pretence of having a dispute to decide; and, while Tarquin was listening to the one who stated the case, the other struck him down with an axe. The Queen however defeated the scheme by giving out that Tarquin was not dead, and sending Servius to administer justice in his name. By the time that the truth became known, the cause of Servius was secure; and he became King of Rome.

The architectural works of Tarquinius Priscus, chief among which were the Great Sewer (*Cloaca Maxima*) and the Great Race-course (*Circus Maximus*), were more important than either his wars or his political institutions.

The great work of Servius Tullius was the elevation of the Plebs to the rights of citizenship. At the beginning a distinction had been drawn by Romulus between Patrons and Clients; but gradually the Aventine Hill had come to be covered with the huts of a multitude, drafted from time to time into the city, especially during the Latin wars of Ancus, but not placed upon a level with the earlier inhabitants. Dividing the Roman territory into about twenty sections or tribes, Servius permitted the Plebeians to meet for discussion in public assemblies called *Comitia Tributa*, just as the Patricians were used to meet in the *Comitia*

Curiata. And to a great national assembly, called *Comitia Centuriata*, and composed of both Patricians and Plebeians, were gradually assigned nearly all the great political privileges, which had once been monopolized by the *Curiæ*.

Servius married his two daughters to the two sons of Tarquinius Priscus, in the hope that such an arrangement would please all and prevent disputes about the succession. And, to make matters still more secure, he mated them by opposites, giving a fierce wife to a gentle husband and *vice versa*. But the fierce ones were not content; and they murdered their gentle consorts. So Lucius Tarquinius Superbus became the husband of the wicked Tullia. This was but one step in their nefarious plot. The next was directed towards the throne. Seconded by the Patricians, who were angry at the elevation of the Plebs, Lucius went and seated himself on the throne at the door of the Senate-house; and, when King Servius came and asked him, how durst he assume that seat, he replied that it was his father's throne, and gave the old man a push which flung him down the steps. While Servius, stunned and bleeding, was striving to stagger home, some of the adherents of Lucius ran after him, killed him, and left his body lying in the street. Tullia, who knew what was going on, drove in her car to the Senate-house to salute her husband as King. But he sent her home at once. At the foot of the Esquiline the driver of the car saw a prostrate figure in the way, and on a nearer approach perceived that it was the King, lying dead. Reining in his horses, he was about to turn aside, when the unnatural daughter, with curses and hard names, perhaps with blows, bade him drive on, nor heed the body. And so over the figure of the slain King jolted the heavy wheels, and then, blotched with bloody stains, went rolling on, staining the stones of the Wicked Street for ever with a horrid memory and name.

The general character of the reign of Tarquinius Superbus, seventh and last King of Rome, was oppressively tyrannical, not only in his treatment of the Plebeians but also in that of the Patricians by whose aid he had gained the crown. In his wars and foreign policy he was successful; but his efforts to obtain absolute despotism made for him many foes, and prepared the way for the great revolution, by which his reign and the Roman monarchy were brought to an end.

He had a son Sextus, by whose means the Latin town of Gabii was taken. Pretending to have quarrelled with his father, the prince fled for refuge to this town, where he was welcomed and made commander of the army. By getting the better of old Tarquin in some skirmishes he secured the confidence of the Gabians. And then he sent a private messenger home to ask for advice. The King said nothing, but walked up and down the garden, switching off the heads of the tallest poppies with a stick. Sextus, reading the hidden meaning, cut off by death or exile the chief men in Gabii; and the undefended city fell an easy prey to Rome.

It was owing to the wickedness of this same Sextus that the Tarquins were banished from Rome. During the tedious siege of Ardea the princes were wont to meet at night to drink wine and talk together; and one evening a dispute arose as to the comparative worth of their wives. "Let us go and see how they are now employed," said Collatinus, a cousin of the Tarquins. So they took horse and rode through the darkness, first to Rome, where they found the princesses in the tumult and glare of banquet-rooms; and then to Collatia, where sat Lucretia, wife of Collatinus, calmly and cheerfully busied among her maidens with the distaff and the carding-comb. To her the princes gave the palm. But Sextus gazed at her with unholy eyes. And, some days later, he intruded himself upon her household as a guest, and despite the welcome he received, made this pure matron the victim of his lust. Lucretia then sent in haste for her father and her husband; and in their presence, having told the tale of shame, slew herself with a knife, crying with her last words for revenge on Sextus.

There was present Junius Brutus, a member of the Tarquin family, who had long been feigning imbecility as a safeguard against the King's jealousy, and who indeed had got his surname from this circumstance. But, as the legend tells us, there was a substratum of tact and talent below his apparent dullness. Having been, a short time before, sent with two of his cousins to consult the oracle at Delphi, he heard a response that the chief power in Rome was to be his, who should first kiss his mother. So, upon the Italian shore, having just left the ship, he managed to have a lucky stumble, and kissed *mother Earth*, by which he got the advantage of his companions.

This man, drawing the red knife from Lucretia's breast, swore revenge upon the Tarquin family, and the bloody blade passed from hand to hand, as the words of the oath from lip to lip. In the market-place of Collatia the body of Lucretia was placed, to rouse the anger of the townsmen by the "poor dumb mouth" of its wound. And, hurrying to Rome, Brutus, who was Tribune of the Celeres, or commander of the cavalry, called an assembly of the people, who, upon hearing the story, agreed to banish the wicked Tarquins. Old Tarquin, when the tidings reached him, rode to Rome, but found the gates closed **509** against him. Meanwhile Brutus had reached the B.C. camp at Ardea, and had won over the army there. The-deposed King took refuge at Cære in Etruria, while Sextus sought safety at Gabii.

CHAPTER II.

THE TARQUINS IN EXILE.

The New Government.
Brutus and his Sons.
Death of Brutus.
Horatius and the Bridge.

Mucius Scævola.
The Swimming Girls.
The First Dictator.
Battle of Lake Regillus.

MONARCHY being overthrown, a Republic was then established in Rome. Instead of a King, ruling for life, two magistrates, elected every year, and bearing the simple name of *Consuls* or Colleagues, were to govern the State. The first Consuls were Brutus and Collatinus; but the latter, being a Tarquin, was soon obliged to retire in favour of Valerius. The emblems of consular dignity and power were three—the toga with a purple hem, an ivory throne called the *curule* chair, and the *fasces*, or twelve bundles of rods with axes inside, which were carried by guards called *lictors*.

The first attempt to restore the Tarquin was set on foot by his envoys, who came to Rome to ask the restitution of his private property. The two sons of Brutus were involved in the plot, which was discovered by a slave who overheard the talk of the conspirators. Among the earliest public acts of Brutus was therefore the dreadful duty of condemning his own sons to death. Crushing down in his heart the natural affection of a father, he bade the lictors slay those who would betray their country, and winced not to see his own blood flowing under the axe.

Before long he had followed his sons to the grave. The people of Tarquinii and Veii having taken up arms for the exiled King, a Roman force, commanded by the Consuls, advanced to meet them. Before the battle there was a fatal duel. Aruns Tarquin, seeing Brutus at the head of the horse, rode at him with lance in rest, much as Bohun rode in a later field at Bruce; and Brutus, better horsed than

Robert of Scotland was to be, couched his spear, and galloped to meet the advancing foe. So fierce was the onset and so true the aim of both, that each drove his spear through the heart of the other; and both sank dead upon their steeds. In the battle that followed there was no decisive success on either side; but a voice at night adjudged the victory to Rome, and the enemy retreated.

Thus baffled a second time, Tarquin had recourse to Lars Porsenna of Clusium, lord of the twelve Etruscan cities, who raised a great army and marched to Rome. The wooden bridge that spanned the Tiber was almost gained, and within the city all was terror and confusion, when a brave man named Horatius Cocles, with two others, Lartius and Herminius, faced the whole Etruscan host at the entrance of the narrow bridge, and slew all who dared to cross swords with them, while, behind, the axes of the Roman were hewing at the beams. When the structure was tottering to the fall, the companions of Horatius escaped across its shaking planks; but it fell with a mighty crash into the flooded stream, before Horatius could follow. In that moment of terror every eye was fixed upon the hero, who stood amid the corpses of the slain, alone in front of many thousand foes. He stayed only to utter a short prayer to the river-god, and then plunged into the yellow flood, which foamed over his helmet, and at first seemed likely to whirl him after the broken spars to the sea. But he struggled through in spite of wounds and weariness, and was received on the safer side with shouts and applause.

Before Porsenna left the Janiculum, a hill overlooking Rome from the Etrurian side of the Tiber, two other instances of Roman hardihood and daring had occurred.

A young Roman of rank, named Mucius, having made a resolve to kill Porsenna, went across the river, and saw a man of noble presence and rich dress paying the Etruscan soldiers. Believing this to be the King, Mucius struck a dagger into his breast. But it proved to be only an officer deputed by Porsenna to pay the men. Dragged before the angry chieftain, the Roman was menaced with death by fire, if he would not confess. "See," cried he, thrusting his left hand into the flame, which wavered on an altar close by, "how weak the torture of flame is to wring a secret from a Roman." And when, in admiration of his bravery, the Etruscan spared his life, Mucius announced that three hundred Romans had sworn to make the attempt in which he had failed. Ultimately Porsenna subdued Rome, and ten girls and ten youths of the noblest in the city were given as hostages to him. One of the maidens, Cloelia by name, plunging into the Tiber and calling on her companions to follow, led the way through the waters back to Rome. The Romans sent her back; but Porsenna, not to be outdone in generosity, gave her freedom, and permitted her to choose the youngest boys to return with her to Rome. Porsenna then went home.

The fourth and last effort to restore the Tarquins was the most formidable of all, for the thirty Latin cities united under a Dictator.

The Romans also appointed a Dictator, who acted as general-in-chief during six months, and, unlike the Consuls, was not required to give an account at the end of his term of power. Lartius was the first Dictator of Rome.

499 B.C.

Two years later, under another Dictator, named Aulus Postumius, the Romans met a Latin army beside Lake Regillus in the territory of Tusculum. The battle consisted, like all these old fights, mainly of a series of single combats. First, old Tarquin, clad in complete armour, engaged the Roman Dictator, but was wounded in the side. There was then a duel between the Latin Dictator and the Roman Master of the Horse. On the whole, the Romans had the worst of the struggle, until Postumius promised a temple to the great twins Castor and Pollux, if they would give him aid. He had scarcely spoken, when two giants of exceeding beauty were seen on his right hand, riding upon snow-white horses. Then the tide of battle turned. Titus Tarquin was slain; the Latins broke; and their camp was carried by storm. But no trace was seen of the giant horsemen, except the print of a single hoof on a rock. That same day the loungers in the Roman Forum saw two young men on white horses, both riders and steeds all stained with bloody dust and the sweat of toil, ride up to a well by the

Temple of Vesta; and from these strange visitors, as they washed the traces of war away in the pure cold spring, the people heard how a victory had been won at the Lake Regillus over the Latin host.

Tarquin's hopes were now over, and he had lost all his sons, for Sextus was slain at Gabii. Retiring to Cumæ on the Bay of Naples, he died there a short time after this defeat.

CHAPTER III.

TRIBUNES OF THE PLEBS.

State of the Plebs.	Menenius' Story.
A piteous Tale.	Tribunes appointed.
The First Secession.	Their Powers.

THE next five chapters will contain an outline of the struggle, which continued for nearly a century and a half, between the Patricians and the Plebeians of Rome, resulting in the admission of the latter to the chief offices in the State.

The first great step in the strife was the movement, by which the Plebeians secured for themselves special magistrates, called Tribunes of the Plebs.

It must not be imagined that the Plebeians at this time were the mob or rabble of Rome. They were chiefly yeomen, who cultivated small patches of land in the Campagna or fertile plain by the city. They were too proud to engage in trade or handicraft of any kind. During the Tarquinian Wars they were forced to take the field every summer; and, being unable like the Patricians to obtain substitutes, or to have their lands tilled by dependents, their fields were neglected, or, if they managed by neighbours' aid to raise a crop, it was often burned or cut down by the enemy during their necessary absence. Thus many of them fell into poverty and debt, borrowing money at heavy usury from the rich Patricians. This opened the door for much oppression; for the Roman law of debt was very severe, permitting creditors, in case of default, to imprison, sell into slavery, or even kill a wretched debtor, and cut his body to pieces.

One market-day the buyers and sellers in the Forum were startled to see in their midst an old man, wretchedly thin, with tangled hair and beard, and covered only with a scanty patchwork of rags. As the chains clanked on his wasted limbs, he told how he had been flung into

THE FIRST SECESSION. 13

prison for debt by a Patrician creditor, and had borne the scars of the whip in his dungeon. He was recognized as a brave old soldier, and the popular wrath rose high, as he recounted his losses in the late war, when the foe had burned his house and wasted his fields. So fierce was the outbreak of Plebeian rage, that the leader of the Patricians, Appius Claudius, was forced to hide himself.

About that time a Volscian War began. But the Plebeians refused to take the field in obedience to the call of the Consuls; nor would they take the military oath, until Servilius, the head of the moderate party in the Senate, proclaimed that imprisonment for debt should be suspended for a time, and that, when the war was over, he would try to have the law changed. Trusting to this, they took the field, and defeated the Volscians. When this had happened twice, without any improvement of their condition, the Plebeians took a decided step; and, choosing two leaders from among themselves, marched with their weapons to a hill, two miles off, where the Anio joined the Tiber. This eminence, from the events that followed, came to be commemorated in Roman history as the *Sacred Mount*.

494 B.C.

The more sensible Patricians sent a deputation to speak to the seceders, who had expressed their resolve to found a new city, where they had encamped; and old Menenius Agrippa, adopting the parable form of address, amused the Plebeians with a short story, telling them how, once upon a time, the different parts of the Body, growing indignant with the laziness of the Belly, which they had to carry about and supply with food, resolved to strike work. The legs stood still; the hands refused to hold or work; the teeth would not chew; and all the other organs joined in the revolt. But the rebels soon found their mistake; for, receiving no nutriment from the Belly, they grew weak, and only too late perceived how much they depended on that great centre of sustenance.

Struck with the point of this parable, as applying to the case between the Patricians and themselves, the Plebeians proposed an arrangement, which was in the main ultimately agreed to. Those debtors, who could not pay, were to be relieved from all liability. Those, who had been reduced to slavery, were to be set free. But a more important feature in the transaction was the appointment of two officials called Tribunes of the Plebs, who were to be chosen from the Plebeians, and whose great duty was the protection of their order against oppression.

The number of the Tribunes of the Plebs was afterwards increased to five, and at length to ten. At first elected by the Comitia of the Centuries, that is, by the Patricians and Plebeians together, they came to be elected by the Plebeians alone, in their own assembly called *Comitia Tributa.* During their year of office the persons of the Tribunes were held sacred; and the most potent weapon they wielded in opposing the Patricians was their right of saying *Veto* (I forbid it) to certain laws or decrees of the Senate, which did not please them. This little word, which could be uttered without assigning any reasons for its use, was almost in itself enough to paralyze the hand which had smitten the Plebs so sorely. Besides the Tribunes, two other Plebeian officials, called *Ædiles,* whose chief duty was to inspect the houses and the streets, were appointed at this time.

CHAPTER IV.
PATRICIAN HEROES.

Coriolanus—the Fabii.	Cincinnatus.
Patrician Legends.	The Camp at Cremera.
Coriolanus.	The Valley of Algidus.
The Agrarian Law.	

IN the legends of the wars, which intermingle with the story of intestine struggle in Rome, the names of certain heroes who distinguished themselves are very prominent. That these legends were the composition of Patrician minstrels is evident from the fact, that the men commemorated are of the upper class.

A certain haughty young Patrician, who by valour at the storming of Corioli had added Coriolanus to his name of Caius Marcius, proposed, when famine was pinching the poorer classes, and corn-ships had come from Sicily, that the Plebeians should be forced to give up their Tribunes, if they got a supply of food. So great was their rage at this that they summoned him before the Comitia, but he chose to leave Rome rather than take his trial. Attus Tullius, a Volscian of Antium, finding this celebrated foe of his race seated by the hearth in the posture of a suppliant, received him hospitably, and with him planned a war against Rome. But the Volscians were unwilling to break the existing treaty. Tullius therefore, upon the occasion of the Great Games at Rome, gave false information to the Consuls that the Volscians, who had crowded into the city, meant to make a sudden attack. The Senate, acting upon this, ordered every Volscian out of Rome before sunset. When Tullius met the throngs of his countrymen, smarting under this ignominious dismissal, he found no difficulty in fanning their rage into intentions of actual war.

Coriolanus was appointed one of the generals of the Volscian army. His old grudge was manifested by the fact that, as the army advanced towards Rome, the fields of the Plebeians alone were ravaged. The foe had come close to the city, when the terrified Senate sent a deputation of five Patricians to beg for peace. Coriolanus sternly told them that he was now a Volscian, not a Roman, and demanded concessions so great as the price of peace that the deputies were obliged to return unsuccessful. A procession of priests, clad in their sacerdotal robes and armed with all the sanctity of their office, availed as little to turn away his sword. But another effort was successful. A train of weeping women, accompanied by the mother of the exile, his wife, and his two boys, approached his throne; and the lofty remonstrances of his aged parent, seconded by the tears and clinging caresses of the others, melted his resolution. "O my mother," cried he, "thou hast saved Rome, but lost thy son;" and in a short time the order to retreat was given.

This step is said to have cost him, first his popularity, and then his life: for Tullius excited the Volscians against him, and he was killed by the angry people.

In the year 486 B.C. a Patrician named Spurius Cassius proposed what is known as an *Agrarian Law;* that is, a law to divide those public lands, which had been the domain of the Kings before their expulsion, among the Plebeians. The Patricians did not decidedly reject the law; their policy, successful for many a day, was to baffle the execution of it. Spurius Cassius, who deserved well of his country for many things, especially for the Leagues he formed with the Latins and the Hernicans, was brought to trial and beheaded; even his very house was levelled to the ground. Foremost in the persecution of Cassius were the great *gens* of the Fabii, by one of whom, Kaeso, the accusation had been made. But the Fabii afterwards supported the Agrarian Law, and desired that it should come into effect; and, when the Patricians still refused to allow this, they all, to the number of three hundred and six, not including their clients, emigrated to a camp on the brook Cremera, lying between Rome and her old foe Veii. For more than a year they did good service by withstanding the hostile attacks of the Veientines, who however watched their opportunity and cut them off by a surprise, when they were going to sacrifice on the Quirinal Hill at Rome on a sacred day in February.

The legend of Cincinnatus is another story framed for the praise of the Patrician order.

One day five horsemen came spurring into Rome from Mount Algidus to tell how the Consul Minucius was beleaguered in a narrow valley by a host of the Æquians. It was an emergency requiring a Dictator, and none seemed fit for that great post but Lucius Quinctius of the curling locks, as the added name of Cincinnatus signified. Living quietly on a little farm across the Tiber, he saw the Senators, who had been deputed to offer him the chief command, approaching one day as he was labouring in his field, dressed only in his tunic. It took some little time to wash himself and put on his toga. When he heard of the pressing need for action, he went at once to Rome, and, ordering all business to cease, summoned every man of military age to the Campus Martius before sunset, enjoining each to bring twelve strong stakes and food for five days. Starting before dusk, the army reached the critical spot about midnight; and at once, by order of the Dictator, set to work at surrounding the enemy, having first announced their arrival to their hemmed-in countrymen by a loud shout. Hearing the hopeful cheer, the army of Minucius made an attack upon the Æquians, and so engaged their attention that the other Roman force worked away all night at trench-digging and palisading without interruption. When day broke, the Æquians finding themselves in a trap between two Roman armies, were obliged to surrender, and to acknowledge their subjection by passing under the yoke, which consisted of a skeleton gateway, made with three spears. Cincinnatus, having accomplished this speedy deliverance of his country, carried the golden crown, with which his countrymen rewarded his skill and valour, back to his rustic home, and settled down again to the humble toils of a rural life.

CHAPTER V.

THE DECEMVIRS.

The New Code. | Second Year.
The Ten Appointed. | Story of Dentatus.
First Year. | Story of Virginia.

A TRIBUNE, named Terentilius Arsa, proposed in the year 462 B.C. that a code of written laws should be drawn up for the settlement of the troubles in the State. It was a Plebeian movement; and during the ten years it took to carry the measure the Patricians endeavoured to turn the Commons from their purpose by various concessions of a less important kind. They increased the number of Tribunes from five to ten, and parcelled out the Aventine among the poorer classes for building-ground. But the Plebeians, by always for many years returning the same men as Tribunes, showed their resolution to succeed. In 454 B.C. the Patricians gave way so far as to permit three men to travel through Greece for the purpose of collecting the laws of Solon and other legislators as a basis for the new Roman Code.

When these men returned to Rome, by the consent of all parties the Consular government was set aside for
451 a little; and Ten Men (*Decemviri*) were chosen
B.C. from the Patrician order to arrange and frame the laws. This was done in peace; and before the year of the Decemviral office had come to an end, ten great plates of copper, engraven with the Roman laws, were set up in the Forum opposite to the Senate-house; and the national assembly of the Centuries sanctioned the enactments of these Ten Tables.

The work of legislation not being yet complete, however, it seemed necessary to continue the Decemvirate for another year. Appius Claudius, the leading man of the Ten, contrived that he alone of the original Decemvirs should be re-elected; and obtained for his colleagues a number of insignificant persons, among whom were some Plebeians. He then commenced a career of oppression, of which his conduct in the previous year had shown no indications. Two additional Tables, making the complete number twelve, were added during this second term of the Decemviral office; but these consisted mainly of laws favourable to Patrician sway, and were added by an edict of the Ten.

By the Code of the Twelve Tables the tribes, that is, the Plebeians, lost jurisdiction in capital causes; but to make up for this "it was enacted that in future every magistrate (and therefore the Dictator among the rest) should be bound on his nomination to allow the right of appeal: if any one should nominate a magistrate on any other terms, he was to expiate the offence with his life." It was now that the Tribunes obtained in full that right of *intercession* or *veto*, to which allusion has been already made. A seat for them was placed at the door of the Senate-house, so that they could hear the debates without being actually in the house.

The Decemvirs did not, as was expected, lay down their office at the conclusion of the second year. The State was then beset by two hostile forces—the Sabines and the Æquians—in the course of war with whom occurred events, which overthrew the oppression of these magistrates.

In the Roman army despatched to fight the Sabines, there was a veteran centurion, named Siccius Dentatus, who had received an extraordinary number of honours and rewards for his bravery. He was the hero of one hundred and twenty fights, and of his forty-five wounds not one was in the back. Having acted as Tribune of the Plebs, he had incurred the anger of the Decemvirs, who, as the legend states, perhaps with truth, took advantage of the war to have him slain. Appointed to command a reconnoitreing party, he found himself assailed in a glen by the soldiers he was leading. The old lion stood at bay with a rock behind him; and his sword drank the blood of many of the murderous crew, before a heavy stone, hurled from above by a coward who had crawled up the crag, crushed him to the earth. The uproar in the camp, when the truth became known, could be appeased only by a splendid funeral.

A yet more tragic interest hangs round the story of the young Virginia, whose piteous fate Macaulay depicts in one of his noble Lays. This lovely girl was the daughter of a brave centurion, Virginius, then serving in the army against the Æquians; and was betrothed to Icilius, a Tribune of the Plebs, who had taken a leading part in the strife between the orders. The tyrant Appius Claudius, smitten with an unholy passion for this maiden, gave secret instructions to one of his clients, who seized her one morning on her way to school, and claimed her as his slave. Thus Appius thought, with a two-edged blow, to gratify his evil desires, and take a bitter revenge upon Icilius. But the device recoiled upon himself. Claudius the client clamoured loudly to have the claim brought before Appius the Decemvir: and in the absence of Virginius with the army, Icilius and the girl's uncle appeared to plead her cause. That afternoon two messengers sped to the camp on Algidus, twenty miles off;—one to Virginius from Icilius, telling the tale and urging him to come to Rome; the other from Appius to the Decemvirs in command, desiring them to refuse leave of absence to Virginius, in which case Virginia, now out on bail, would have been delivered to him who called himself her owner. The message to Virginius reached the camp first, and he hurried to Rome.

449
B.C.

Next morning the case came on in the Forum. Virginius and his daughter, in mourning dress, appeared in the centre of a sympathizing crowd. Claudius stood almost alone, except for the lictors, who surrounded the tribunal. In spite of her father's presence, Appius adjudged Virginia to be the property of Claudius, and commanded the lictors to aid him in taking possession of her. Then in his heart Virginius formed a desperate resolve. Begging permission to say a few words to her in private, he took her to that side of the Forum where a butcher kept his stall; and, snatching a knife from the block, struck it into her heart. Then, with the red blade in his hand, he rushed through the crowd, which opened to let him pass; and, reaching the gate safely, rode off to the camp with the dreadful news.

FALL OF THE DECEMVIRS.

The army followed him to a man; the other army joined in the revolt; and the Commons in the city, having pelted and hustled Appius from the Forum, flocked to the Aventine, where the Plebeian soldiers had erected their banners.

But it seemed fit to the Plebeians, who made Duilius their leader, to withdraw to the Sacred Mount, the scene of the former secession. And there they received a deputation from the Senate, to acquaint them with the fact that the Decemvirs had been forced to resign, and to receive the terms on which they proposed to negotiate. The principal condition the Plebeians insisted on was the restoration of the Tribuneship with a complete right of appeal against the power of the supreme magistrate. As to the "Wicked Ten," Appius and Oppius, being thrown into prison, committed suicide, while the others went into exile.

CHAPTER VI.

CAMILLUS AND THE GAULS.

The Struggle continued.
Siege of Veii.
Battle of the Allia.
Gauls in the Forum.

Geese Save the Capitol.
The Weighing of the Gold.
The Tore and the Crow.

THE interval between the fall of the Decemvirs and the siege of Veii, at which the great Camillus distinguished himself, is filled with the narrative of successive steps in the Patricio-plebeian struggle, each resulting in favour of the latter order. First, in 445 B.C. was passed the Canulcian Law: by it was enacted, that "marriage between a Patrician and a Plebeian should be valid as a true Roman marriage, and that the children of such a union should follow the rank of the father." The same year witnessed the passing of an Act, which ordained that sometimes instead of Consuls there should be elected, from Plebeians as well as Patricians, six Military Tribunes with consular powers. When the Patrician order saw this successful assault on the supreme power, they broke it up in order to prevent the Plebeians from ever enjoying it all. The chief step taken towards this end was the appointment of two Censors, nominated from among the nobles for a term of eighteen months. These officers, besides certain duties connected with taxation and public works, exercised a power over all classes, and could depose for immorality persons of the highest rank.

How vindictively the struggle was carried on, may be judged from the treatment of Spurius Mælius, a rich Plebeian, who during the famine of 440 B.C. sold corn at a cheap rate to the starving people. He was accused of aspiring to be King; and old Cincinnatus was called forth in the departing twilight of his life to act as Dictator in crushing this formidable man. Summoned before the Dictator's tribunal, Mælius refused to obey; upon which

Ahala, the Master of the Horse, slew him in the Forum in open day. His house was razed; and his stores of grain were distributed for nothing among the people, —perhaps for the purpose of appeasing that wrath, which must have boiled within them, when they saw the blood of their benefactor reddening the dust of the Forum.   **439 B.C.**

The sharpest struggle, which Rome had with any of the neighbouring cities, was that with Veii, lasting ten years (406-396 B.C.) This town, situated about twelve miles off, engaged in a war with Rome for the defence of Fidenæ, which however was taken and destroyed. Veii was then invested by a Roman force; but the Roman soldiers, unused to siege-work, let summer after summer pass away without making any impression on the defences. The need of keeping the field during the whole year caused an arrangement to be made, by which now for the first time the Roman soldiers received pay from the public chest. At last, in the seventh year, a strange omen happened. The Alban Lake swelled up so as to overflow the brim of its basin, and pour down upon the lower ground: and, as the oracle and the soothsayers had declared, that Veii should not fall until its waters sought the sea, the Romans cut a tunnel through hard rock to the Anio, and thus fulfilled the prophecy. Furius Camillus had in the meantime been appointed Dictator at Rome. While the beleaguered Veientines saw no change in the blockade, which still surrounded their city, the Roman engineers, under the direction of Camillus, were secretly cutting a passage under the walls towards the foundation of the citadel. So close, it is said by the legend, did the miners come at last to the surface that they distinctly heard the voice of a Veientine soothsayer tell the King, who stood ready by the altar, that whoever completed the sacrifice should be victorious in the struggle. The earth trembled, and broke; and out of the chasm leapt Camillus and his men, who rushed to the shrine and slew the victim.

The massacre of the citizens and the fall of the city followed; and white-robed youths bore with bloodless hands to Rome the statue of the great goddess Juno. So fell Veii, the Troy of Roman legend, after a ten years' siege.   **396 B.C.**

The Patricians permitted an Agrarian Law to pass, by which the lands of Veii were distributed. Camillus however, partly by his Patrician pride, and partly by an injudicious proposal he made to take a tenth of each man's plunder for an offering to Apollo, incurred the bitter wrath of the Plebeians. Charged with appropriating the bronze gates of the city that had fallen before his prowess, he was obliged to leave Rome, and took refuge in the Latin town of Ardea.

But retribution was at hand. Hordes of yellow-haired giants, with fierce blue eyes and skin liker to northern snow than the dusky olive of the south, had poured over the Alps, and were even now climbing the Apennines to descend upon the Tiber basin. These were the Senones, a tribe of the wide-spread race called Celts or Gauls.

When the invaders appeared before the Etruscan city of Clusium, the affrighted inhabitants sought aid from their ancient foes in Rome. Three ambassadors of the Fabian Gens were sent to warn the northern tribes that an assault upon Clusium would draw down upon them the vengeance of Rome. Little caring, the barbarians engaged in a battle, during which one of the envoys was seen stripping a Gallic chief whom he had slain. This enraged the Gallic leader Brennus so much, that he marched at once towards Rome.

On the banks of the brook Alia, a tributary of the Tiber from the Sabine Hills, the barbarian host was stopped for a time by a Roman army in battle array. Brennus **390** succeeded in forcing the position by turning the B.C. right flank; and the Tiber grew thick with Roman dead, either drowned in flight or slain with Gallic spears. When news of this disaster reached Rome, there was hurry but no panic. The Patricians of military age retired to the rocky Capitol; the Plebeians and the women went chiefly to Veii, now luckily lying empty for their reception ; while the priests with the sacred images and vessels betook themselves to Caere. But a nobler band than all—those grey-haired men who had served in the Senate and had borne the Consular and Censorial dignity—feeling that their unstrung arms could not avail any longer to defend their country, resolved to await the coming of the foe. And, when the barbarians, pouring tumultuously but not without caution and suspicion through the open gates of Rome, came to the Forum, their voices grew hushed in awe, for there in the centre of the meeting-place before the temple of the gods, on ivory chairs, whose adornments were half hid by flowing robes of white and purple, sat men reverend with snowy beards and furrowed brows. Memories of their own Druids, pontiffs of the oak-forest, must have grown thick under the shaggy thatch of the Gallic heads, when the unexpected scene disclosed itself; and one of the foremost approached a seated figure, and put forward a fearful hand to stroke the white cataract of beard. The seeming statue raised an ivory truncheon, and struck the savage to the ground. This broke the spell of awe. The figures were of men, not gods: and the Forum was soon strewed with silver-haired dead.

The siege of the Capitol then began, and went on for seven months, at first during scorching days, which thinned the Gallic ranks with plague and fever. Once, says the legend, the rock was in imminent danger of being scaled. A venturesome youth, bearing a message from Veii, had climbed the steep rock, where it descended towards the river; and the Gauls, not unused to mountaineering, traced out his hazardous path by rocky shelves and little jutting shrubs. By night in single file a band of them tried the same way of ascent; and the foremost had actually swung himself almost to the highest ledge, without attracting the ear of the sleeping sentinels, when some geese in the Temple of Juno, which even pinching famine had not induced the beleaguered Romans to kill, began to cackle and flap so violently, that a Roman named Manlius awoke, just in time to see the danger, and hurl the Gaul down the rock.

Tired of the siege, the Gauls agreed to go, if they got one thousand pounds' weight of gold. This was collected; and they hurried away to repel an invasion of their territory in Northern Italy by the Venetians. The inventor of the legend, in order to gloss over the fact that Rome did really pay a tribute to the Gauls, made up a pretty story to the effect that deliverance came just at the critical moment, when the gold was in the scales, and Brennus had flung his sword in among the weights in order to increase the amount of the tribute, and insult the submitting Romans. Camillus, it is related, came from Veii at the head of an army, desired the gold to be taken back to the Roman chests, for not gold (he said) but iron should redeem the city. And then, falling on the astonished Gauls, he drove them from the place and slew them to a man.

The Gauls came back in smaller numbers on at least two subsequent occasions, which are celebrated in the legends of Torquatus and Corvus. In a duel fought at the Anio Bridge in 361 Manlius slew a Gallic giant, and took from his neck the *torc* or twisted collar of gold, which indicated royal or princely rank. And in 349, when, on the Volscian plains, a tall Celt was vapouring before the armies, and daring any Roman to single combat, Valerius accepted the challenge and advanced to fight. Just then a crow lighted on the head of the Gaul, and, clinging to his hair, with claws perhaps entangled in the uncombed mass, flapped its wings and pecked at his eyes so fiercely as to make the victory of the Roman easy. Hence these champions were named—the one Manlius *Torquatus*—the other Valerius *Corvus*.

CHAPTER VII.

THE LICINIAN ROGATIONS.

The City Rebuilt.	Victory of the Plebs.
Fate of Manlius.	Temple of Concord.
Licinian Rogations.	Steps gained by Plebs.
Details of the Strife.	

THE seven months spent by the Gauls before the Capitol, reduced the city of Rome to a mass of ruins. There was accordingly much talk about removing to Veii, where the Plebeians had already been established for some time. But the chance words of a centurion, directing his banner to be fixed in the Forum, were accepted as an omen; and, bringing materials from Veii, the Romans began to raise a new city amid the mounds of rubbish that represented their old homes. A patched-up and very crooked city it was, which grew out of these heaps: and there was neither good drainage, good ventilation, nor much beauty in the Roman streets for centuries afterwards.

The need of building new houses, and the stoppage of all farming operations plunged the Plebeians into new debts, and the old evils were beginning to appear, when Manlius, the defender of the Capitol, stood forth as the champion of the lower orders, selling his land to pay the debts of those who were about to be imprisoned. This of course exposed him to the charge of aiming at regal power; and there arose a struggle between him and the Patricians, whom he accused of embezzling some of the gold raised for the Gauls. Not being able to prove this, he was imprisoned, and then brought to trial before the Centuries. In the Campus Martius, surrounded by those whose debts he had paid, he exhibited the spoils of his sword, the scars on his breast, and pointed to the rocky Capitol, where he had saved Rome. Seeing that the vote would be in his favour on that spot, his enemies dissolved the assembly; and by a meeting, held where the Capitol could not be seen, he was condemned to death. He was flung from the Tarpeian Rock (384 B.C.).

Eight years later began that movement, which resulted in the complete victory of the Plebeians.

Two Tribunes of the Plebs, Licinius and Sextius by name, brought forward three Bills, which with a fourth afterwards added are known in Roman history as the Licinian Rogations. They were—

376 B.C.

I. That of all debts, on which interest had been paid, the sum of the interest paid should be deducted from the principal, and the remainder paid off in three successive years.

II. That no citizen should hold more than five hundred jugera (about three hundred and twenty acres) of the Public Land, and should not feed on the public pastures more than a limited number of cattle under penalty of fine.

III. (And most important.) That henceforth Consuls, not Consular Tribunes, should be elected: and that *one of the two Consuls must be a Plebeian*.

IV. (Added five years afterwards.) That instead of two Patricians (the Duumvirs) being chosen to keep the Sibylline books, there should be *ten* men, taken from both orders.

Sensible that the critical struggle had now arrived, the Patricians bent all their energies to defeat these demands. And their hands were strengthened by the fact that the richer Plebeians had strong objections to the first two laws, which would entail heavy losses on them. Licinius and Sextius, driven to desperate measures by certain of their own colleagues, who opposed them, put their *veto* on the proceedings of the great National Assembly, so that the State was left without her chief magistrates for five years. In vain the Senate appointed Dictators: they could do nothing. Then compromise was tried. The Patricians allowed the fourth Rogation to pass, and promised to pass the first two, if the third were struck out. To this the Tribunes would not listen: and the struggle continued five years longer, when the Patricians gave way; and the Rogations became law, after a contest of nearly ten years.

367 B.C.

In the following year (366 B.C.) L. Sextius was chosen the first Plebeian Consul. The Patricians at first refused to confer the sovereign power, which could be conferred only by their special assembly. But by the advice of Camillus, now made Dictator for the fifth time, they yielded this point, on condition that the judicial power should be taken from the Consuls and put into the hands of a Patrician magistrate called *Prætor Urbanus* (Prætor of the City). They also further divided the Consular power by creating a new office, called the *Curule Ædileship*.

Though the strife was now really over, and a Temple of Concord, vowed by Camillus but not dedicated by him, for death intervened, arose in the Forum—an emblem in stone of the equalization of the orders, and the hoped-for union of the nation—yet for a while there continued to be Patrician struggles and impediments, gradually however weakening and melting. Step by step the victorious Plebeians won successive places in the government of the State—gaining the Dictatorship in 356—the Censorship in 351—the Prætorship in 337—and last of all, in 300, that admission to religious office, so jealously guarded as to be last won, the right to hold the sacred stations of Pontiff and Augur.

SECOND PERIOD.

CHAPTER I.

THE SAMNITE AND LATIN WARS.

Curtius.	Latin War.	Third War.
The Samnites.	Second War.	Battle of Sentinum.
First War.	Caudine Forks.	

ROME was now, from the abatement of violent intestine conflicts, able to look abroad and prepare for the reduction of all Italy. She passed through an ordeal of plague, of which Camillus died, and underwent other misfortunes from floods and earthquakes. A great chasm having opened in the Forum, the Augurs said that it would not close, until the most precious things in Rome were cast into it; upon which Curtius, dressing himself in full armour, spurred his horse to the brink, and leapt in, crying as he did so that Rome's riches lay in brave men. They say the gulf closed, and swallowed what may be regarded as almost the last of the Roman legends.

Among the mountain valleys lying north of Campania, dwelt a nation akin to the Sabines, and bearing the name of Samnites. After the manner of Italian mountaineers they led their flocks higher and lower, as the season changed: and from their rocky nests among the Apennines they sent out frequent swarms of settlers, who occupied the seaward plains. It so happened that most of these became Greek in their habits, and were sometimes at war with their old mountain home. Chief of these emigrant bands were the Campanians, who took Capua and Cumæ, which they made centres of their power. In fact, under various names the Samnites at this period had spread themselves over all

Southern Italy, but their centres were loosely connected, and independent. Greek cities lay scattered here and there in their dominions. Rome had a great advantage in her compact territory.

The First Samnite War lasted two years—from 343 B.C. to 341 B.C.

It arose out of an attack which the mountain Samnites had made upon the Campanians in consequence of the latter aiding an Oscan tribe. Capua sought the aid of Rome; and in order to appease the Roman scruples against making war with allies, as the Samnites were, the inhabitants agreed to surrender their city to Rome.

Valerius Corvus and Cornelius Cossus were the Consuls of the year. The former defeated the Samnites at Mount Gaurus, near the watering-place Baiæ: the latter and his legions were saved from destruction by the valour of a Plebeian, Decius Mus, who got possession of a hillock and extricated his countrymen from a perilous pass. The second year was unnoted for any great event in the war, which was brought to a close in consequence of difficulties between the Patricians and Plebeians, and a hostile spirit which was springing up between the Romans and Latins. This feeling ultimately developed into a Latin War (340 B.C.—338 B.C.)

The cities of Latium proposed a union with Rome, which was to continue the centre of government. The conditions favourable to themselves asked by the Latins were, that one Consul should always be a Latin, and that three hundred Latin members should be added to the Senate. Manlius Torquatus swore that he would slay the first Latin who crossed the threshold of the Senate-house; and a Latin envoy, who spoke irreverently of the great Roman god, fell down the temple steps and was killed. The Romans rejected with contempt the proposal of union.

Manlius and Decius Mus led the Roman armies to the war, of which the chief event was the battle of Mount Vesuvius. Two incidents related of this conflict are most characteristic of Romans in that age. The one concerned the son of Manlius, who, leaving his post to fight and slay an insolent Latin, in spite of his father's strict orders that none should stir from the ranks, was put to death for disobedience by command of that stern disciplinarian and hardhearted parent. The other was the self-sacrifice of Decius. Some dreams having troubled the Consuls, they agreed that he whose division gave way should offer himself to the infernal deities. The troops of Decius were beaten back in the battle, upon which their leader prepared to die in due religious form. Wrapped in a toga (which was the garb of peace, not war) he stood upon a spear, and in a loud voice doomed himself and the foe to death. Then at the full speed of his horse he pierced the enemy's line, and quickly met the death he sought. The Latins, frightened by the deed which seemed to secure godlike aid to their foes, broke and were defeated: all the more readily, when the fresh troops of Manlius, kept in reserve by a stratagem, which made them think they had already fought the third battalion, poured upon their wavering ranks. The Latins took the field no more; but held out in their cities for two years longer.

Thus Rome acquired dominion over Campania and Latium.

A peace of twelve years led to the Second Samnite War (326 B.C.—304 B.C.) The Roman aggressions on the River Liris had long been exciting a bitter feeling among the Samnites; but the immediate occasion of the war was the siege of Palæopolis on the Bay of Naples, which the Romans undertook, because the city refused to give satisfaction for injuries inflicted on Roman subjects. Samnium gave aid to Palæopolis: and so the war began. It lasted twenty-two years: during six of which (321—315) the fate of Rome seemed to be certain disaster and destruction. But her star rose again brighter than ever.

The glorious disobedience of Fabius, the Master of the Horse, whom the Dictator, Papirius Cursor, when recalled to Rome, had left in command with strict orders not to fight, but who did nevertheless fight and win a splendid success, is the most striking feature of the earlier war. Vainly Papirius, who was only a rough and ignorant man, notable chiefly for his physical qualities of swiftness and hardiness, strove to punish the victorious Patrician. The temper of the army and of the citizens generally would not permit Fabius to suffer.

THE CAUDINE FORKS.

The Samnites were soon so humbled as to sue for peace: but the terms offered by the Senate were too severe: and the war continued.

But a great captain now appeared among the Samnites to change the aspect of affairs, in the famous Pontius, distinguished not only as a soldier but also as a scholar.

As the Roman Consuls were marching through the Apennines towards Apulia, they were caught in a trap at the Caudine Forks. Passing through a narrow defile they reached a little plateau, of which another pass formed the outlet. Pontius held the latter, and, when the Romans tried to retrace their steps, they found a second Samnite force in possession of the entrance. In vain they strove to cut a passage through: the loss of one half of their officers compelled them to seek for terms. Pontius agreed to let the whole army go, upon acknowledgment of submission and surrender of their officers and their arms, if the Roman leaders would consent to secure a favourable treaty. This being agreed to, the Roman soldiers, stripped of their upper clothing, walked sullenly in single file beneath the yoke. And great gloom fell upon all Rome in consequence of this ineffable disgrace. But by refusing to sanction the treaty, even after the Consuls had signed it, the Romans contrived to continue the war.

321 B.C.

A defeat at Lautulæ seemed to augur ill for the Romans; but their losses were soon retrieved by a victory, which prevented the Samnites from taking the field, until the adhesion of the Etruscans gave them new strength. Then they put forth mighty efforts. But the Roman sword was too heavy. A Samnite army, gorgeously equipped with gilt and silvered shields, was defeated by Papirius Cursor, the Roman Dictator; and they were so exhausted by their unavailing struggles, that they did not engage in battle again during this war. Piercing the thick Ciminian woods, Fabius invaded Etruria, and defeated the Vulsinians utterly near Perusia. These events induced the Samnites to sue for peace, which was granted.

The Third Samnite War lasted from 299 B.C. to 290 B.C.

After a devastating invasion of Samnium and a counter-rush by Gellius, a brave Samnite, into the valley of the

Tiber, the great battle of Sentinum in Umbria was fought. There was arrayed a vast allied host of Samnites, Umbrians, and Gauls, collected for a last vigorous effort to crush the threatening pride of the city by the Tiber. A Roman force of sixty thousand men confronted them, under Fabius Maximus, and Decius Mus, son of the other hero of that name. Ever on the look-out for omens, the two armies, before the battle began, watched a wolf that chased a hind between the lines. The hind ran among the Gauls, who slew it: the wolf passed unharmed through the Roman ranks, who saw in the presence of a beast like that which suckled Romulus a sign of good fortune. Then the battle began. The wooden cars of the Gauls were new to the Romans, and for a time threw them into confusion, upon which young Decius devoted himself exactly as his father had done, and with the same effect. Fabius, having routed the Samnites, came up in time to aid the Roman division of Decius in defeating the Gauls. This was the decisive battle. There were others during the five years of lingering war that followed: and at last Pontius was taken prisoner. The submission of Samnium followed. But the Romans sullied their victory by beheading the brave and wise old man, who had treated their soldiers with such noble generosity at the Caudine Forks.

295 B.C.

CHAPTER II.

THE CAMPAIGNS OF PYRRHUS.

Tarentum.	Battle of Asculum.
Battle of Heraclea.	Pyrrhus in Sicily.
Cineas.	Defeated at Beneventum.

THE success of Rome in these Samnite wars excited the jealousy and fear of the Greek cities in Southern Italy, one of the chief among which was the great Lacedæmonian settlement of Tarentum. A neighbouring city named Thurii, being attacked by the Lucanians, obtained aid from Rome; and in the course of their operations ten Roman galleys, in spite of a treaty with Tarentum, sailed into the gulf on which that city stood. The Tarentines, collected at noonday in the theatre, looked from their seats and saw the venturous squadron. At once they rushed to the shore, launched their ships, and sank four of the Roman vessels. This hostile act was followed by a march to Thurii, and the sack of that town.

Well aware that Tarentum was the secret soul of a vast Anti-Roman league, which embraced Samnites, Lucanians, Etruscans, and other Italian nations, and somewhat tired of war, the Romans at first sent envoys to Tarentum to ask quietly for explanations. They arrived during a feast of Bacchus, when the populace were full of wine. When the leader of the embassy, Postumius by name, began to speak in Greek, the mob roared with laughter at his strange accent and his blunders in grammar. This he did not care for: but, when a low fellow threw filth upon his toga of pure white wool, he lifted the stain in sight of all the people, and in a voice of thunder warned them that it would take their best blood to wash the insult out. A war then began: and the democrats of Tarentum invited Pyrrhus, King of Epirus, to come over and help them.

When Pyrrhus arrived with an army of about twenty-five thousand men, he began at once to turn the luxurious Tarentines into soldiers by shutting their theatres and baths, and subjecting them to constant drill. In spite of their murmurs they were obliged to yield to this unpleasant change.

281
B.C.

In the plain of Heraclea on the banks of the River Siris Pyrrhus met a Roman army for the first time. It was memorable as the first meeting of the Phalanx with the Legion. A Greek army was then arranged in one or two solid masses, many men deep, and forming a complete hedge of bristling pike-points: while the Romans fought in three lines, called *Principes, Hastati*, and *Triarii*, which made their attack in succession. In vain the triple wave of Roman valour flowed on the rocks of Grecian steel. Neither javelin nor sword availed to gap the serried fronts. The Roman horse gained a trifling advantage over the Thessalian squadrons; but, when Pyrrhus brought up his twenty elephants, with dark trunks curling and snorting, and ponderous feet shaking the earth in a swift but clumsy trot, the Romans fairly turned their backs and fled, appalled at the new kind of *oxen*, which Pyrrhus had discovered in Lucania. Recovering their order, they then fell back upon Venusia.

When he had walked over the field of Heraclea, and had viewed the Roman dead with wounds all in front, Pyrrhus felt that it would be wellnigh impossible to conquer men who fought so well. He therefore resolved to send the eloquent Cineas to Rome to offer peace. This great orator appeared before the Senate, and spoke skilfully for his master; but the blind old Censor Appius Claudius, being led down to the House, convinced the wavering Fathers that there was only one condition on which Rome could treat, and that was—the immediate departure of Pyrrhus from Italy.

When Cineas returned and told Pyrrhus how he had failed, the fiery soldier rushed through Campania and Latium, and never stopped until within eighteen miles of Rome. But the Latins did not join him. It was during this winter that the Roman Fabricius, whom gold could not tempt, came to Pyrrhus concerning an exchange of prisoners. The Greek, having failed in bribery, tried to play upon the envoy's fears by suddenly withdrawing a curtain and disclosing a huge elephant, which waved its trunk over the head of Fabricius. But the Roman never winced.

The second campaign of Pyrrhus was signalized by a defeat of the Romans at Asculum under circumstances similar to those of Heraclea. Convinced that victories over Roman soldiers were too dearly bought, and startled by the news that Rome had concluded an alliance with Carthage, Pyrrhus sought an opportunity of making peace. An instance of Roman generosity afforded this chance. A physician sent secretly to the Roman Consuls, offering to poison the Grecian King. They rejected the base proposal; and sent the intended victim word, for which he was so grateful that he set free all the Roman prisoners without ransom. And then he crossed into Sicily (278 B.C.) to make war against the Mamertines and the Carthaginians.

He remained in Sicily nearly three years, during the first portion of which he was brilliantly successful: but reverses came. Cineas died. A failure in the siege of Lilybæum followed; and he evacuated the island.

Misfortunes then began to thicken. The Carthaginians destroyed part of his fleet as he was sailing to Tarentum. And, after having taken Locri, he laid violent hands on the treasures in the Temple of Proserpine, to whose wrath superstition ascribed the loss in a storm of the ships that carried the booty.

The final battle of the Pyrrhic War was fought at Beneventum in Samnium, where Curius Dentatus commanded the Roman forces. Pyrrhus made a night-march in the hope of surprising the enemy; but his soldiers lost their way; and the wearied battalions were assailed in the morning by the Romans, who were fresh and vigorous. The dread of the elephants had also worn off, and the Romans baffled the monsters by shooting at them arrows headed with blazing tow. which drove them back furious with pain. The defeat of Pyrrhus was complete: he departed from Tarentum, where however he left a garrison under an officer named Milo.

275 B.C.

This soldier of fortune died ignobly about two years afterwards at Argos, struck by a tile which a woman flung from a house-top.

CHAPTER III.

THE FIRST PUNIC WAR.

Cause of the War.	Regulus.
First Roman Fleet.	Siege of Lilybæum.
Mylæ and Ecnomus.	Battle of Ægusa.
Invasion of Africa.	Peace.

ROME thus became mistress of Southern Italy. There was indeed what was called a Fourth Samnite War in 268 B.C.; but it lasted only a year.

As Pyrrhus was leaving Italy, he uttered words prophetic of a struggle between Rome and Carthage, a great maritime colony of Tyre, which had existed for many centuries on that angle of the African coast which runs nearest to Sicily. In fact the Romans and the Carthaginians had already become slightly embroiled during the Tarentine war: but now a more decided occasion of hostilities arose out of the troubled affairs of Sicily.

Carthage had long been spreading her dominion over the neighbouring islands and coasts. Sicily, Sardinia, Corsica partly, even the Balearic group, and the shores of Spain had been seized by her far-stretching grasp. But in Sicily she took a special interest, it being nearer and richer than the rest. Of the Greek cities there, Syracuse was her most formidable opponent: but in spite of resistance the Carthaginians made good their footing in the triangular island. It so happened that a Syracusan tyrant brought over to help him in his wars a band of Campanian mercenaries: and after his death these Mamertines or "men of Mars," as they called themselves, seized the town of Messana, whose position made it the key of Sicily. The Syracusans attacked Messana, one portion of whose garrison invited over Roman aid, while the other admitted Carthaginian soldiers. The Romans came, drove back the Syracusans, expelled the Carthaginians, and found themselves engaged in a war, which lasted three-and-twenty years (263 B.C.—241 B.C.). This contest is known as the First Punic War, from the name *Poeni* (adjective *Punicus*), by which the Romans styled the Phœnician colonists who occupied Carthage.

When the two Roman Consuls appeared in Sicily at the head of a splendid army of fifty thousand men, it seemed good to Hiero of Syracuse to make peace with Rome; and he continued to be her faithful ally for nearly half a century. The Romans invested the strong city of Agrigentum in 262. For seven months the siege continued, the besiegers being themselves surrounded by a hostile force. But the Romans were ultimately victorious. The Carthaginian leader fled by night, and the garrison were butchered.

But Carthage could not be conquered on land alone. The Romans had ships; which however were not large enough to cope with the Punic five-deckers or quinqueremes. It was therefore necessary to build a fleet and train a number of sailors. The former the Romans did by copying the lines of a Carthaginian ship, stranded upon the Brutian coast; the latter was accomplished by erecting scaffolds on the shore, and drilling the rowers to pull to the measured sound of flutes, as if they were actually sweeping the sea with their oar-blades. Sensible however that they could not vie with the trained Carthaginian mariners in such manœuvreing as was necessary to drive the iron-spiked prow with fatal accuracy into an enemy's side, the Romans had at the prow of their ships drawbridges with hooked ends, which they lowered at close quarters. Pouring in their marines, they thus turned the action into a species of land-battle.

The efficacy of this expedient was soon proved. The Consul Duilius with his new ships met a Punic fleet off the headland of Mylæ, north-west of Messana, and by dropping the gangways on each as it came up, contrived to secure or destroy about fifty vessels. In honour of this signal success a column, bristling with the beaks of the Carthaginian ships, was set up in the Roman Forum.

260 B.C.

The moral effect of this victory was great; and most of the Sicilian towns, except a few great centres, soon afterwards yielded to Rome.

The Senate then resolved to carry the war into Africa. Under Regulus and Volso, the former of whom bears a distinguished name in Roman history, a fleet of three hundred and thirty sail left the southern coast of Sicily, having on board, between sailors and soldiers, fully one hundred and forty thousand men. A Carthaginian fleet of greater size, and at least as fully manned, rode the waves at Ecnomus in a single line. The Roman ships, 256 placed in the form of a wedge, broke the line at B.C. once; and the *crows*, as the bridges were called, did the rest. Though beaten, the Carthaginian fleet fell back in tolerable order towards the African coast.

The Roman army then landed unhindered in the Bay of Clupea, on whose shore they formed an intrenched camp. Victory seemed certain; for wealthy towns submitted on all sides; and the Numidians rose in revolt against Carthage. By a most short-sighted policy the Senate withdrew the greater portion of their army, leaving not twenty thousand men under the command of Regulus. With these he advanced towards Carthage, whose energies seemed to have undergone sudden palsy, and formed his camp for the winter at Tunis, only twenty miles distant from the great Punic capital.

So humbled were the Carthaginians that they sued for peace; but Regulus asked for Sicily and all their island-possessions in the Western Mediterranean, and proposed such humiliating terms as to their navy that their crushed spirit rose; and they resolved to renew the war rather than submit to his degrading demands. The winter brought them aid of various kinds, among which were the services and advice of Xanthippus, a Spartan captain of mercenaries, who had found his way to Africa.

Regulus meanwhile seemed to have lost his wits. He neglected to secure a line of communication with his camp at Clupea. He despised the aid of a light cavalry force, though he might easily have collected such among the Numidians, who were proverbial for their horses and their horsemanship. He trusted entirely to Roman discipline and Roman steel— admirable things when used at fair odds and with common precautions. In a plain near Tunis was fought the battle, which ended at a blow this Roman invasion of Africa. The first charge of Carthaginian horse, under the direction of the Spartan, scattered the handfuls of Roman cavalry, which hung like tiny cloudlets on the two wings; and at once the Roman army was outflanked. The Legions on the left pressed forward victoriously; but the right and centre, with horse behind and elephants in front, were obliged to throw themselves into the form of a square. The waves were too many and too fierce for the rock. It shook—tottered—broke—melted. The dead heaped the plain; a poor two thousand reached Clupea; and Regulus was carried a prisoner to Carthage.

255 B.C.

The Roman fleet, defeating the Carthaginians off the Hermæan headland, rescued the remnant of the army at Clupea; but on its way to Syracuse there fell on it a storm, so sudden and fierce, that the sea was strewed with dead and driftwood. The Romans had now no fleet.

Three months however repaired the loss; and with three hundred sail they attacked Panormus on the Sicilian coast, and took possession of the place. Disaster still hung over their navy. A second storm burst, and swept away the greater portion of the new fleet, filling the minds of the Senate with such gloom that they resolved to keep only sixty ships at sea henceforth.

For two years there was a lull in warfare, until the Carthaginian general Hasdrubal marched against Panormus, within which lay the Roman Proconsul Cæcilius Metellus. The Punic army was strong in elephants; and against these the Roman bowmen and slingers directed their missiles. Some of the wounded beasts fell into the moat; others, wild with pain, went trampling furiously back upon their own ranks. All was confusion, amid which the Proconsul made a decisive attack, driving the foe to the margin of the sea. The Carthaginians lost one hundred and twenty elephants; and soon found themselves reduced to the possession of only two Sicilian towns—Drepana and Lilybæum.

250 B.C.

It was then, according to a romantic tale, upon which

sober history casts some doubt, that an embassy proceeded from Carthage to Rome, accompanied by Regulus, who had given his solemn promise to return to his prison, if peace were not obtained. The captive general, smarting under a sense of his degradation, refused to enter the gates of Rome, or take his seat in the Senate. When some of the Fathers came out to ask his opinion as to the granting of the peace, he boldly declared his voice to be for the continuance of the war, until Carthage was destroyed. And he then went back to a horrible death. He was thrust into a barrel studded inside with sharp nails. His eyelids being cut off, the bloody and unprotected orbs were exposed to the copper glare of the mid-day sun; and so he was left to perish, without a drop of water to cool his black dry tongue. But his name is written in the bright roll of patriot-martyrs; and the greatest pens of his country took delight in recounting the noble serenity with which he turned away from the tranquil joys of home to face the unknown terrors of his African dungeon.

Having built a third fleet, the Romans undertook the siege of Lilybæum, investing the place by land, and blockading its port by sea. In spite of all the Roman vigilance, however, the Carthaginians managed to throw supplies of both food and men into the beleaguered city. This year was disastrous to the Romans. The Patrician Consul, an arrogant Claudius, made a foolish attempt to surprise the Carthaginian fleet in the harbour of Drepana; but succeeded only in so huddling his own ships together in a confined space that they were easily destroyed. So careless was he of the spirit of his men, that when word was brought to him before starting that the holy pullets would not feed, he answered flippantly, "Not feed! then let them drink!" and tossed the coop overboard. *We* may smile at the incident; but in days when men trusted much to omens, the effect of such conduct was very dispiriting. To make matters worse, a storm completely shattered the rest of the Roman fleet and a large squadron of food-ships and transports, as they were trying to find shelter on the coasts of Gela and Camarina. Thus perished another—the third—Roman navy.

249 B.C.

During several years the Romans remained without ships, and the war degenerated into skirmishing in Sicily. It was conducted on the side of Carthage by a young general, famous on his own account, but yet more famous for the son he gave to history in the person of the great Hannibal. Hamilcar, who bore the surname of Barca, signifying lightning, took possession of two mountains, Hercté overlooking Panormus and Eryx near Drepana, whence he harassed the Romans, kept up communication with the sea, and drew in supplies from the surrounding country. Being defeated in one of the slight encounters, that were constantly occurring, Hamilcar asked the Roman Consul to make a short truce that he might bury his dead. The Consul rudely replied that he ought to mind the living rather than the dead. Some time later, the Romans were obliged to make a similar request, which Hamilcar granted at once, adding the gracious words " that *he* warred not with the dead, but with the living."

At last the Roman spirit rose—not in the Senate, where feeble counsels still prevailed, but among the rich citizens, who saw Roman privateers successful on the seas, while Rome had no national navy to fight her battles. By means of subscription a splendid fleet of two hundred ships, including the corsairs and their trained crews, was equipped, and presented to the State by a patriotic band. And with this Lutatius Catulus went to sea.

His first movement was upon Drepana, which he blockaded, and where he received a wound. The Carthaginians were unable to send ships to the relief of the place until the following spring; and then they sent rather a cluster of transports than an organized fleet of war-vessels. The Roman officer, who acted for the wounded Consul, intercepted the Carthaginian ships near a little island called Ægusa (now *Favignano*), and, forcing them to fight, won a decisive victory, sinking fifty and capturing seventy of the enemy's galleys.

241 B.C.

The battle of Ægusa brought peace, which the Carthaginians, and especially the merchants among them, had been longing for. After crucifying the admiral who lost the battle, the Punic authorities desired Hamilcar to accept terms. The Consul at first demanded the arms of the submitting force and the surrender of all Roman deserters; but Hamilcar refused to yield these points. Sensibly drawing back from this demand, Catulus then laid down the basis of a negotiation, which, when fully framed and amended by a Roman commission of ten, contained the following leading items :—

1. The surrender to Rome of Sicily and the small islands adjacent.
2. The restoration of all Roman prisoners without ransom.
3. The payment by Carthage for the costs of the war of 3200 talents (£790,000), one-third down, and the remainder in ten annual instalments.

There was then a pause of three-and-twenty years.

CHAPTER IV.

THE SECOND OR GREAT PUNIC WAR.

Illyrian and Gallic Wars.	Fabius Cunctator.	Hasdrubal's March.
Hannibal.	Battle of Cannæ.	The Metaurus.
Siege of Saguntum.	Sieges of Syracuse and	Scipio in Africa.
Hannibal's March.	Capua.	Battle of Zama.
Ticino — Trebia—Trasimene.	Scipio in Spain.	Peace.

DURING the interval between the First and the Second Punic Wars, Rome was engaged in subduing the Illyrian pirates, who under the spirited Queen Teuta had pushed their power even to the conquest of Corcyra. The treachery of her governor Demetrius, whom the Romans rewarded with part of her dominions, obliged her to submit. But the Gallic Wars of this time were far more momentous. The Gauls, whom their defeats at Sentinum and Vadimo had quieted for a time, rose in arms, when a law was passed in Rome to parcel out among the Plebeians some of the lands wrested from them. The Boii, aided by the Insubres, a warlike tribe from Milan, invaded the valley of the Arno; but the great battle of Telamon (225 B.C.) cost them fifty thousand men; while other victories, won upon the banks of the Po, placed all Northern Italy to the very foot of the Alps in the hands of Rome. Strongholds—Placentia (*Piacenza*), Cremona, Mutina (*Modena*),—began to spring up for the purpose of securing the conquered territory.

Turning to Carthage, we find her, immediately on the cessation of the First Punic War, involved in a deadly struggle with her own mercenary troops. Not until 238 did Hamilcar succeed in crushing the mutiny. Rome took no advantage of *this* trouble; but, when something similar happened in Sardinia, she aided the insurgents, and forced Carthage to give up both that island and Corsica.

Hamilcar, who hated Rome with a perfect hatred, and

who was eyed jealously by a faction at home, now formed the project of founding a Carthaginian dominion in Spain. Crossing in 235 B.C. the strait we call Gibraltar, he established in the south of Spain a sort of kingdom, which flourished and grew great. But in battle with the natives, who were fierce in fight, he met his death.

It is about the time of Hamilcar's emigration that we catch the first glimpse in history of his illustrious son Hannibal. The little boy of nine pleaded so hard with his father to be taken to Spain, that Hamilcar yielded, but first led him to an altar and obliged him to swear an oath of changeless hatred and hostility towards Rome. We can well fancy how the dread scene would impress the childish memory, and colour all the aspirations of the growing youth!

Hannibal not being yet old enough to take the lead in Spain, it devolved, when Hamilcar fell, upon Hasdrubal, his son-in-law. This chieftain founded Carthagena, and made a treaty with Rome, by which the Ebro was marked out as the northern limit of the Carthaginian territory in Spain. In the seventh year of his rule he was assassinated.

Hannibal, then in his twenty-ninth year, was elected by the officers to the chief command. He had undergone a special training for his great career. From earliest childhood his mind had been familiar with the chances of war with Rome—his oath we have already heard of—few men could beat him in running, boxing, or riding—and neither want of sleep nor want of food seemed to weaken his iron frame. To such physical advantages he added the important one of possessing a well cultivated mind; and, after becoming a general, devoted himself so steadily to Greek that he became able to write that master-language. His genius as a tactician will speak for itself. In inventive craft—in suddenness of action, pouncing on the enemy when least expected, having advanced by some unusual route—in the quick knowledge of men and movements, which he contrived to obtain, not only by his own keen penetration, but by a far-reaching system of detectives and spies—in his extraordinary power of attracting to his standard men of many minds and various speech—

220
B.C.

he resembled beyond all others the Corsican soldier of our own age.

Soon overrunning Castile, Hannibal made the Punic power in Spain actually extend to the banks of the Ebro—with the exception of one spot, the city of Saguntum (*Murviedro*). The siege of this city was the immediate occasion of the Second Punic War. When Hannibal commenced this enterprise, which cost him eight months, Roman ambassadors came into his camp to intercede for the city, which was an ally of Rome. But he refused to grant their request. **219 B.C.**

When tidings came to Rome that Saguntum had fallen, an embassy proceeded to Carthage to demand that Hannibal should be given up, as one who had violated the law of nations. The Carthaginians refused to make any such sacrifice, upon which a Roman, with that fondness for dramatic effect characteristic of Southerns, held up a double fold of his toga, crying, "In this fold I carry peace and war: choose ye." "Which you will," was the bold reply. "Then war be it," said he, shaking the drapery out.

The welcome news soon reached Hannibal, in whose busy brain a daring project took shape. He resolved to invade Italy from the North. Between Carthagena, his headquarters, and the basin of the Po, lay four great natural obstacles—two great rivers and two mighty mountain-ranges. But this was not all. Fierce and unknown tribes occupied the ground; and the perils, which had seemed comparatively insignificant to a handful of scouts, sent out to survey the proposed route, were magnified a thousand-fold, when the transport of an army with all its needful appendages came to be provided for.

In the spring of 218 B.C. the memorable march began. With ninety thousand foot, twelve thousand horse, and fifty elephants he moved to the Ebro, where the natives resisted his approach. These were easily brushed aside; and in a little while the great granite peaks of the Pyrenees pushed their points into the sky, while his army paused under their shadow. Symptoms of discontent had already begun to show themselves on account of the unknown regions, into which the general was now **218 B.C.**

evidently leading his men : but Hannibal met this difficulty by simply disclosing his project in all its grandeur, and permitting those who did not wish to proceed, to go home. About eight thousand left him there.

He did not climb the Pyrenees, but turned the eastern point of the chain ; and so passed on towards the Rhone by way of Narbonne and Nimes, marching through regions either friendly or afraid.

The current of the Rhone presented the first serious obstacle. The Roman general Scipio, who had been at Pisa, preparing to embark for Spain, heard of Hannibal's march and directed his course to Massilia (*Marseilles*), for the purpose of disputing the passage of the river. But he did not calculate on the rapidity of the march ; and lingered by the sea, while Hannibal was floating his men across at Avignon. Though the Romans were not there, a hostile force of Gauls lined the further bank. The two days necessary to collect boats and make rafts were, however, also sufficient to carry a cavalry force up the river to a safe place for crossing. And, when Hannibal saw a thick smoke rising behind the Gauls, he knew that his horsemen were there. Seizing this moment, he commenced to carry his army over. For a short time the Gauls resisted ; but soon the sight of their tents on fire, and the foe behind, turned them from the river. They were easily beaten then. The elephants were decoyed, it is said, upon rafts strewn with earth and leaves, and were thus towed across in safety. Hannibal then marched up the valley of the Rhone to the Island of the Allobroges, north of the Isere. Scipio did not follow, fearing the unknown country ; but, sending his brother and the troops to Spain, he returned to Pisa.

In the Island of the Allobroges, a region between the Rhone and the Isere, Hannibal rendered some service to a Celtic chief, who repaid him with supplies. The army then met the first mountain-wall of the Alps, dividing the upper from the lower Isere. Unfriendly Celts beset the pass, which Hannibal was forced to seize in the night : but the descent was not accomplished without much slipping of mules and horses, and ceaseless attacks of the mountaineers. The valley of Chambery afforded a wider and pleasanter scene for the march. In the narrowing defile the tribe Ceutrones advanced to meet Hannibal with branches and garlands and kine. He accepted but distrusted their offered kindness; and accordingly, when he entered the rugged gorge leading upward to the St. Bernard, he took the precaution of sending his baggage forward with the horse, while he kept the foot behind to cover the march. It was well he did so. For suddenly every rock to right and left appeared alive with foes, who mustered also in great force behind; and from the sloping sides of the pass the Ceutrones sent great stones rolling down upon the climbing threads of men. At the White Rock, a mass of snowy chalk, which sprang from the very root of the St. Bernard, the Carthaginian general halted his infantry and faced the foe, while the horses and the baggage-mules toiled up the pass. Resting by a little lake upon the watershed, he then began to descend, slightly troubled by human foes, it is true, but obliged to face perils of various kinds. Here, a sheet of sloping ice powdered with new snow and ending in the edge of a crevasse, from whose intensely blue depths no skill could extricate—there, a precipice, whose side sank in a wall sheer down for thousands of feet. A cry or the cracking of a whip would bring an avalanche tumbling on the road, blocking up or tearing away the precarious shelf, on whose perilous zig-zag they crawled down the face of the mountain. Then the intense cold—the ceaseless toils—the sinking hearts—all combined to render the march one of misery. But their troubles were now almost over. Following the course of the Doria, which sprang from the lake by which they had rested, they found the path growing every day easier, the valley wider and more fertile. The cold blue glare of ice—the deadly still whiteness of the spreading snow—and the dark gloomy fringe of firs changed by pleasant gradations into the soft foliage of olive and chestnut and the glowing gold of the Italian plains. The last fortnight of September, spent in thorough rest at the village of Ivrea, restrung the worn warriors, and prepared them for the toils of battle.

Thus was the greatest march of ancient times accomplished. Let us count the cost. The review at Roussillon had displayed a force of fifty thousand foot and nine thousand horse: among the hamlets of Ivrea were scattered scarcely twenty thousand foot and six thousand horse, but many of the latter horseless. And the elephants were sadly thinned, as well in number as in size.

The passage of the Alps had taken fifteen days—the whole march from Carthagena to Ivrea, somewhat less than four months.

At this time the two Roman armies were both far away —the one in Spain, the other in Sicily. There was but a small force in the basin of the Padus (*Po*), and these had enough to do in curbing the restless Gauls. Hannibal's first achievement was the capture of Turin, the capital of the Taurini. Scipio advanced with all the men that could be hurriedly mustered to check his advance down the river. The first collision was a skirmish chiefly of cavalry, between the Ticino and the Sesia, in which Hannibal's Numidian horse gained the day. Scipio was severely wounded in the action; and here his son, most illustrious of the name, starts nobly to life on the historic page, as we behold him, a boy of seventeen, rushing amid the hostile squadrons that he might turn their weapons on himself and so save his father.

By recrossing the river and then breaking down the bridge Scipio gained time to take up a strong position near Placentia, covered in front by the Trebia, which, though a shallow stream in summer, was now brawling with winter rain. Hannibal crossed the Po by a bridge of boats, but meanwhile the second Roman army had arrived, and the northern force now mustered nearly forty thousand men. It was the policy of Sempronius, the Consul in command, to wait; that of Hannibal, to fight; and the latter gained his object by a stratagem. Early one December morning he sent

218 his Numidian cavalry across the river to skirmish
B.C. with the Roman light troops. Meanwhile he hid

a body of two thousand men in a ravine thick with underwood and reeds, and commanded all his troops to take a good breakfast and rub themselves with oil, as a defence against the cold. The Carthaginian horse, feigning flight, dashed through the icy stream; the Romans pursued, wading breast-deep through the torrent, and half blinded by the piercing sleet that blew in their faces. The main body followed, when they saw the danger of their comrades; and, with hands benumbed, shivering limbs, and empty stomachs, were obliged to face the fresh, but not fasting, lines of Hannibal. The Roman infantry did wonders of valour; but, when Mago, Hannibal's brother, led his men from the reedy hiding-place upon their rear, the Legions broke and fled. The first division, numbering ten thousand, forced a way obliquely through the enemy to Placentia; but numbers perished in the Trebia and on its banks. The victory, however, cost Hannibal all his elephants but one; and many of his soldiers caught diseases of lung or limb from exposure, which brought them to their graves.

Thus Hannibal became master of Northern Italy. When the winter had passed, he penetrated the Apennines, and came down upon the basin of the Arno. The floods were out upon the marshes, and the army was forced to march for four days through snow-water. The horses' hoofs rotted off them with disease; the soldiers died in numbers; and Hannibal himself, riding on his solitary elephant, lost an eye from acute inflammation.

But consolation awaited him. The Roman Consul, a popular but self-conceited Plebeian, named Flaminius, lay at Arretium, intending, when the waters fell, to blockade the Apennine gorges. Hannibal passed him by, moving towards Perusia. The Consul followed hastily, and fell blindly into a trap. Beside the Lake Trasimene there is a defile with two steep walls, along which Hannibal disposed his men. A thick mist from the reedy lake overhung all the low grounds, as Flaminius led his army into the pass. The vanguard suddenly heard the noise of conflict behind, but could see nothing. "There was no battle; it was a mere rout." Fully fifteen thousand Romans fell on the field. So fierce was the struggle that the shocks of a great earthquake attracted no notice amid the clang and excitement of battle.

217 B.C.

Terror prevailed in Rome. But Hannibal did not approach the city. Drawing his army off through the Apennines into Picenum, he spent the heat of summer there; and in the cooler season marched into Apulia, where his cavalry revelled so freely in wine as sometimes, it is said, to bathe their horses in grape-juice. He then pushed westward through the Apennines by way of Beneventum, and directed his march towards Capua. Meanwhile an eagle eye watched him coolly from the heights; and, ever as he moved a Roman army, keeping well out of reach, followed him, cutting off his supplies and troubling him by petty attacks. This was the plan adopted by Fabius, the newly appointed Dictator, whose tactics earned for him the surname of *Cunctator* (The Lingerer). As Hannibal descended the Vulturnus, withering by his ravages the rich vineyards that produced the amber Falernian, this cautious general closed the passes in his rear and waited. When Hannibal, finding that the Capuans would not revolt, desired to return to Apulia, he was obliged to resort to stratagem in order to obtain an open road. Finding a Roman force blocking the way, he collected a great herd of oxen, and, tying lighted torches to their horns, drove them in the dark over the heights that walled the road. The Romans, mistaking these for the Carthaginian army climbing the hills by torchlight, left the pass, through which Hannibal quickly pushed his men. He soon afterwards formed his winter camp at Geronium near Luceria, a flat district of northern Apulia, rich in grain and grass.

217 B.C.

The Romans were much dissatisfied with the slow caution of Fabius, although events that followed proved its wisdom. Hannibal, too, with all his victories, was disappointed, for the Italians were making no effort to rise in his favour, a thing he had calculated on from the beginning.

The new Consuls, from whose energy Rome looked for great results, were Æmilius Paullus, the hero of the Illyrian war, and Terentius Varro, a butcher's son, very popular and very full of belief in himself. Well had Fabius gauged his worth, when he cautioned Paullus, saying, "You will have to contend not only with Hannibal, but with Varro."

In the early part of 216 B.C., Hannibal having seized the Roman magazine at Cannæ, the Consuls proceeded to that place with an army of eighty thousand foot and six thousand horse. Paullus saw that the ground was too favourable for cavalry, and wished to move into a more broken country; but Varro was for an immediate fight. They had sole command on alternate days; and, when Varro's second turn came, he hoisted the red flag on his tent. Well pleased to see this signal for action glittering in the morning light, the Roman soldiers fell into their ranks. They were formed in close order, more like the Greek Phalanx than their ordinary array. Hannibal, quick to perceive an advantage, drew up his allies in a long thin convex crescent, tipped at each horn with a massive column of African veterans. In the opening cavalry skirmish the Carthaginian cavalry were successful. As Hannibal expected, or rather intended, the Roman Legions pushed in his weak centre, and followed up their success. This movement placed them, worn by their contest, between the dense wing-columns, which closed in upon their flanks. The valour of Paullus, displayed in spite of a sling-wound, went far to restore the Roman array; but when Hasdrubal, with his heavy horse from Spain and Gaul, came thundering upon the rear of the legionaries, the confusion of the Romans became irretrievable. There was then a frightful slaughter; the flower of the Roman army lay mangled on the field, from which a bushel of gold rings—the ornament of a Roman knight—was taken by the victors. Paullus died; Varro fled. The pale Tribune, who came riding into Rome with the fatal news, told how the former, sitting wounded on a stone, and refusing all means of escape, had sent a dying message to Fabius, telling him to defend the city.

Aug. 2, 216 B.C.

But Hannibal again avoided a march to Rome, perhaps because he was not prepared for a tedious siege. The people of Southern Italy declared on his side. Some cities indeed held out, such as Neapolis and Cumæ; and at Nola Hannibal met his first reverse. Claudius Marcellus, a veteran general, who had won the *spolia opima* in the Gallic War by striking the King Virdumarus from his horse and slaying him, made a sudden march, threw himself into the city, and repulsed Hannibal in a successful sally. This slight repulse marks the turning of the tide.

But Hannibal was welcomed at Capua, the second of Italian cities, where he took up his winter-quarters. That winter of luxury seems to have disorganized his army, and enervated his hardy troops. Besides, his army was nearly worn out; and, when he sent his brother Mago to Carthage asking for aid, an ungrateful faction gave but a chilling reception to the request, and only very slight assistance was accorded to him—four thousand horse, forty elephants, and a little money.

Meanwhile the Romans, sensible that a worse than Pyrrhus had come, put forth all their energies to prepare for the next campaign.

The war in Italy in 215 B.C. produced no event of consequence. The three Roman leaders, Marcellus, Fabius, and Sempronius Gracchus, occupied intrenched camps and made successful raids, while Hannibal hovered between Campania and Apulia, in the latter of which, at Arpi, he took up his winter-quarters.

Next spring (214) the Romans began their efforts to invest Capua, which Hannibal partially prevented. But they renewed their attempts pertinaciously.

A war with Macedonia, newly allied by treaty to Carthage, here begins to interweave itself with the story of the Second Punic War; but, as it has been already adverted to in Grecian history, it is unnecessary to repeat the narrative here. (See page 122, Grecian History.)

Another episode was the siege of Syracuse, which lasted two years (214–212). Upon the death of Hiero in 216, his grandson, a boy dazzled by Hannibal's glory, succeeded. But he was murdered, as were also his relatives; and two usurpers, mere agents of Hannibal, rising to the surface of the revolution, turned the Syracusans completely against Rome. Marcellus came to besiege the city. For eight months he tried every means of attack; but within the walls the great engineering genius of old Archimedes, the mathematician, directed the defence. Wondrous stories, some true, some fictitious, were related of iron hands, which stooped from the battlements to grasp and overturn a ship —of monster burning-glasses, which shrivelled sails and masts like so much brushwood—of machines that hurled not merely stones but massive rocks heavy enough to sink a galley at a blow. Archimedes obliged the Romans at last to begin a blockade. A Carthaginian army came to the rescue of the place; but the Romans, climbing a part of the wall left unguarded during a feast, took the Upper City; and swamp-fever slew the Punic and Syracusan soldiers, who were camping in the marsh of the Anapus. A Carthaginian fleet, from which aid was expected, turned its prows away. And at last the city was surrendered to Marcellus (212 B.C).

Hannibal's capture of Tarentum in 212 did not compensate for the loss of Capua, which was wrested from him in the following year by Fulvius Flaccus. When the Carthaginian leader saw the fall of Capua imminent, he tried to frighten the Romans into raising the siege by making a dash towards Rome. Pressing along the Valerian Way, past Tibur, to the Anio bridge, he halted within five miles of the walls. But the destruction of a few villas and farm-steadings formed all his achievement; and he turned away, baffled in his hopes that the Romans would desert Capua to defend Rome. Fulvius treated the Capuans with terrible cruelty. **211 B.C.**

Hannibal took refuge in the land of the Brutii, the toe of the Italian boot. In 209 B.C. Quintus Fabius crowned his career by retaking Tarentum—a severe blow to the Carthaginian cause.

The interest of the war now shifts to Spain, whither Hannibal looked eagerly for aid, which he expected his brother Hasdrubal to bring. Under the two elder Scipios the Roman arms were at first most successful in Spain. They pushed their conquests almost to the southern rock we call Gibraltar, and retook Saguntum from the Carthaginians. Their skilful policy also drew to their side an African prince named Syphax, who ruled the coast of Algiers. So much importance was attached to this alliance that Hasdrubal was obliged to leave Spain for the purpose of putting down this turbulent chieftain; a task which he accomplished with the aid of Masinissa, the son of Gela, a neighbour and rival of Syphax.

When Hasdrubal returned to Spain in 211, Masinissa joined his standard. The Scipios, taking twenty thousand Celtiberians into their ranks, were incautious enough to divide their forces. It was easy to bribe the Spanish guerillas: and partly thus, and partly by cutting off the Roman armies from each other, the Carthaginians defeated them in detail, and the Scipios were slain. The Roman authority in

Spain was thus contracted to the Ebro; nor was it without difficulty that Caius Marcius held that line unbroken.

There was difficulty in getting a Roman to take the command in Spain. After much delay a young Military Tribune of twenty-seven, of refined manners, graceful speech, and handsome person, with long hair waving on his shoulders, and modesty crimsoning his cheeks, came forward to entreat the Centuries to send him out to avenge his father's death and save the Roman cause in Spain. Those who looked upon the young soldier, whose gentle mien concealed the courage of a hero, remembered how by the Ticino, while yet a mere child, he had risked his young life to save his father's: and with one accord the voice of the Centuries elected Publius Scipio Proconsul for Spain, 211 B.C.

Finding the three Carthaginian armies of Spain scattered —two on the Tagus and the other at the Pillars of Hercules—Scipio resolved to make a sudden attack on New Carthage, the Punic capital. In this he succeeded **209 B.C.** marvellously. The town stood upon a tongue of land connected by a narrow neck with the main shore. By this isthmus Scipio began his attack, and column after column assailed the wall till noon. In vain. But, while the exhausted garrison were taking their *siesta*, a fresh attack was made. They ran to repel it; and in their haste did not notice a small band of men with ladders wading the lagoon below the harbour-wall, which was quite unguarded. Thus Scipio took the town, in which were vast stores and treasures.

Next year Scipio invaded Andalusia, where he defeated Hasdrubal at Bæcula (208 B.C.). But the wily Carthaginian suffered loss here that he might carry out his cherished plan of tracking the steps of his giant brother into Italy. Disengaging himself, he pressed northward over the Tagus to the shores of Biscay, and penetrated into Gaul by the western gates of the Pyrenees. Scipio knew of his design, and fell back upon the Ebro to dispute the passage; but he was too late. Hasdrubal was then marching towards the Alps. Spain was quickly conquered; Mago sailed to Italy; Gades (*Cadiz*) fell into the hands of the Romans; and the thirteen years' struggle was over. Spain was now a

BATTLE OF THE METAURUS.

Roman province, but by no means a peaceful possession (206 B.C.)

Hasdrubal spent the winter of 208-7 in Gaul. Then, pushing through Auvergne, he crossed the Rhone at its junction with the Isère, and passed over the Alps by the very route which Hannibal had taken, but, owing to the season, with little or no hindrance. He stopped his march to assail the Roman colony of Placentia, and send notice of his arrival in Italy to his brother Hannibal. Nero and Hannibal were then moving their armies through the southern peninsulas of Italy, like wary chess-players full of caution but prompt to take instant advantage of a false move. It so happened that the messengers of Hasdrubal, missing the way to Hannibal's camp, were seized by the sentinels of Nero. With the aid of an interpreter he learned from the intercepted despatches that Hasdrubal meant to advance from Ariminum by the Flaminian Road to Narnia in Umbria, where he requested Hannibal to meet him. Nero, acting on his own authority in the emergency, took a quick resolve, and as quickly put it into action. Choosing seven thousand men, he set out at dusk, as if for a secret raid into Lucania; but he pressed on and on, until at Sena Gallica he reached the camp of Livius, into which he stole at night, the watch-fires of Hasdrubal twinkling only half a mile away. The surprise of the Carthaginian was great, when he heard *two* trumpets sounding the signal in the Roman camp, and saw the greater strength of the lines as they drew out to offer battle. He declined it, and retreated with his troops. The Romans pursued them to the river Metaurus, whose flooded current their ignorance of the fords prevented them from crossing. In the battle that ensued two circumstances decided the victory in favour of the Romans. One was the confusion caused by the wounded elephants; the other was a stratagem of Nero. While his men were actively engaged with the Gauls on Hasdrubal's left wing, he made a detour with a chosen band behind his own troops, and attacked the Spaniards on the right in flank. With a swollen stream behind, the destruction of the army was complete. Hasdrubal died as became one of "the lion's

207 B.C.

brood." Thus ended the battle of Sena or the Metaurus.

Secretly returning to his camp at Canusium, Nero carried with him a ghastly proof of his success—the bloody head of Hasdrubal, which he caused to be flung one morning into Hannibal's lines. This was the first hint of Hasdrubal's arrival that Hannibal had received. It was enough. He retired with his army to the wild and rugged land of the Brutii; while the white horses of a Triumph—a sight long unseen by Roman eyes—stepped proudly over the flowers that strewed the Sacred Way.

It had long been Scipio's design to make Africa the theatre of war; and in spite of factious opposition he carried his point. Sailing from Lilybæum, he landed with a small but well-chosen army at the Fair Promontory near Utica. Masinissa joined him with a few horse. The blockade of Utica was his first undertaking; but the approach of a vast force under Syphax compelled him to spend the winter in a naval camp upon a neighbouring headland. He averted attack by entering into pretended negotiations with Syphax; and, when the spring came, got rid of his foes in one night by a sudden movement, which set in flames the reedy cabins and timber huts in which they were quartered.

204
B.C.

A reinforcement from Spain enabled Syphax and Hasdrubal to continue the contest. Scipio defeated the allied army on the Great Plains, about seventy miles from Carthage. The capture of Syphax added to the disasters of the Africans. Scipio, advancing to Tunis, waited for Carthage to yield.

The city of Dido then sent an embassy to Rome, and at the same time an urgent summons to Mago and Hannibal to hasten to Africa. Mago died of a wound during his voyage; Hannibal came to try, if he could save the thankless country he had not seen for six and thirty years. For sixteen of these he had kept an army together in a hostile land with scarcely any aid from home. No news ever pleased the Romans better than that which told them of the departure of their mighty foe. They rejected the proposals of the Carthaginian ambassadors.

BATTLE OF ZAMA.

Landing at Leptis, Hannibal took up a position on the plain of Zama, probably near Sicca. It was felt on both sides that a crisis had come. Hannibal tried by a personal interview with Scipio to gain better terms than those offered: but in vain. Then the battle began. In the arrangement of his lines Scipio left spaces here and there between the bands of his infantry, so that the elephants, of which Hannibal had eighty, might pass through without disordering the army. Hannibal's third line, formed of his Italian veterans, was his chief hope. Retreating before the elephants, the Roman light troops ran down the lanes left in the army; and the beasts, following, were tortured to fury by the pricking of pikes from each side. Some of them ran right through to the rear of the Roman army; others fell back with deadly trampling on their own ranks. The brunt of the battle was borne by the centres. The first lines remained long locked into a terrible strife, till they retired in exhaustion. Then the second divisions engaged; but there was so much unsteadiness among the Carthaginian militia that the mercenaries turned their swords upon them, and a suicidal combat strewed the ground with dead. Then Hannibal brought up the "Old Guard," upon whom he most depended. Scipio made a fragmentary array to face them, and the most intense struggle of the day began. The veterans never flinched in the face of superior numbers, until Masinissa and Lælius came galloping up with the victorious horse. This decided the day, and annihilated the Carthaginian army.

202 B.C.

Scipio then granted peace to Carthage. The principal terms of the Treaty were:—

1. The Carthaginians were to be left independent within their own territories.
2. They were to surrender all prisoners and deserters, all their elephants, and all their ships but ten triremes.
3. They were not to make war at all beyond the limits of Africa, nor in Africa without the consent of Rome.
4. Masinissa was to be acknowledged King of Numidia.
5. They were to pay to Rome for fifty years an annual tribute of two hundred talents (£48,800).

Scipio then went home to enjoy the splendours of a Triumph, and to wear henceforth the proud name Africanus. The conclusion of Hannibal's story is contained in the narrative of the Syrian Wars.

201 B.C. Rome rested from the struggle of seventeen years, with a diminished population and almost exhausted resources, but with the proud consciousness of having established her dominion firmly over all the shores of the Western Mediterranean, by humbling the only foe potent enough to contest that dominion with her.

CHAPTER V.

THE THIRD PUNIC WAR.

Cato the Censor.	Two Useless Years.
His Triumph over Scipio Major.	Scipio in Command.
Death of Hannibal.	Fall of Carthage.
Delenda est Carthago.	

BETWEEN the close of the Second and the beginning of the Third Punic War a period of fifty-two years elapsed. During this interval were waged the Second Macedonian War, in which Philip was defeated at Cynoscephalæ; the Syrian War, closing with the defeat of Antiochus at Magnesia; and the Third Macedonian War, in which Perseus lost the Macedonian crown on the field of Pydna. An account of these wars has been given in the last of the chapters upon Grecian history.

At home the historical interest of this time centres chiefly in the person of Marcus Porcius Cato, commonly called Cato the Censor. This man was a native of Tusculum, where he was born in 234 B.C. The model, after whom he shaped his style of life, was Curius Dentatus, who, although the conqueror of Pyrrhus and the Samnites, lived frugally on less than seven acres of land, which he laboured with his own hands. Cato, whose grey eyes, red hair, and projecting teeth were not attractive, wore a coarse robe, and prided himself upon disdaining every luxury. This attracted the notice of Valerius Flaccus, a noble neighbour, who induced the rough-spun soldier to devote his energies to the affairs of State. Cato's valour contributed mainly to the victory over Antiochus at Thermopylæ in 191 B.C.

He came into violent collision with Scipio Africanus, at whom he aimed by requiring the brother of the great conqueror, surnamed Asiaticus in honour of his victory over Antiochus, to account for the money spent in the Eastern War. Africanus, tearing the books to pieces in the face of the Senators, expressed his scorn at the petty insinuation of the demand. This contempt of the Senate resulted in an accusation against Africanus, who appeared, richly dressed, on the anniversary of Zama, and by a skilful reference to his great achievement, drew almost all hearts in Rome to his side. But the attack was nevertheless successful. His brother was all but arrested, being saved from that disgrace by the interference of Tiberius Gracchus, who feared a civil war. Africanus then retired to a villa at Liternum, where he died in 183 B.C.

The same year witnessed also the death of Hannibal, who, being expelled from the court of Antiochus after the battle of Magnesia, took refuge with Prusias, King of Bithynia, who sheltered him for some years. But the rage of Rome pursued him thither, demanding his surrender. Prusias was too weak to refuse, so that the hunted lion had no resource but to die. A hollow ring, filled with poison, which he always wore in expectation of such an emergency, afforded him the means of escape from his relentless foes.

After Scipio's retirement, Cato, in spite of senatorial opposition, was elected to the Censorship in 184 B.C.—the crowning honour a political life could receive. In this powerful office, which enabled him to degrade senators and knights for vice, and to inspect the private income and expenses of the citizens, Cato distinguished himself as the unflinching foe of luxury in every shape. Jewels, carriages, rich furniture, costly dress, all fell under his ban. In his stern efforts for the restoration of primitive simplicity and hardihood, he interfered even with sanitary measures, and destroyed the pipes by which private persons conveyed water into their houses from the public fountains. By such conduct he incurred the odium of the rich, but pleased the common people. Against Greek learning he inveighed bitterly; but so far altered his views in his later days as to devote himself to the study of the Grecian literature.

Secretly urged by the Roman Senate, Masinissa meanwhile had been losing no opportunity of plundering the Carthaginian territories. In vain the Carthaginians sought reparation at Rome: they were at last goaded into making reprisals.

OPENING OF THE THIRD PUNIC WAR.

Cato, in extreme old age but with vigour unimpaired, went to Africa as one of a Commission to inquire into the state of affairs between Carthage and Numidia. The sight of a rich and powerful city filled him with jealous alarm. On his return home he represented strongly to the Senate the danger of permitting such a rival to exist. Shaking some Libyan figs, large and bursting with sweetness, from the fold of his toga, he cried to the bystanders, who picked up the fruit with admiring looks, "The place these grew in is only three days' sail from Rome." And every speech he made henceforward ended with the words, "Delenda est Carthago." Scipio Nasica (*i.e.*, Scipio of the sharp nose) opposed him; but Cato's words prevailed. And the Third Punic War soon began.

Rival factions divided and weakened the city of Hannibal. The wealthy merchants advocated submission to Rome; the popular party cried out for war. When the former gained the upper hand, they sent a humble embassy to Rome. But the levies had already begun. Nevertheless the Roman Senate agreed to spare Carthage, if three hundred of her young nobles were sent across the sea as hostages. This was done, yet the fleet of Rome anchored at Utica, and the Legions encamped on the African soil. Another embassy from Carthage was met with a demand for all arms and engines of war. These were yielded up. But, when the Consuls declared that Carthage must be razed, and a new city built at a distance from the sea, the Carthaginian people broke into a roar of fury, and prepared for war. A member of the war-party, bearing the famous name of Hasdrubal, was elected to the command of the Punic forces. So resolute was the spirit of defence that the Carthaginian ladies cut off their long hair to supply material for twisted bow-strings.

The Consuls expected an easy triumph; but they sat with their Legions for a whole campaign before the walls of Carthage without making any impression on the place. Nor were the Consuls of the succeeding year more successful. It was not until the command of the Legions was given to young Scipio, the adopted son of Africanus, who was made Consul at the unusually early

149 B.C.

age of thirty-eight, that any gleam of success began to gild the eagles.

The first care of this young general, who had been serving already under the unsuccessful Consuls, was to enforce rigid discipline among the Legions, and to clear the camp of a mob, that encouraged vice and luxury among the troops. This done, he assaulted and took Megara, the southern suburb of the city, a place of pleasant gardens. Hasdrubal was foolish and brutal enough to kill his prisoners in sight of the besiegers as a reprisal.

147
B.C.

Scipio then drew lines across the isthmus (Carthage stood on a peninsula, shaped like the head of a hammer,) so as to cut off communication with the land. He also blockaded the harbour with his fleet, so that the besieged could get no supplies, except when a strong wind from the sea enabled quick light skiffs to run into the haven, before the heavy Roman vessels could beat out to prevent them. To prevent this method of conveying food to the famished inhabitants, Scipio commenced to make an embankment across the mouth of the harbour. While he was engaged in this difficult and tedious undertaking, the besieged were secretly cutting a new channel to the sea and building a new fleet of fifty ships. The Romans were greatly vexed, when they saw this fleet sailing out of the newly-cut passage; but in a few days they managed to drive the Carthaginian ships back into the outlet and destroy them nearly all in the confusion.

Early in the following year Scipio made a feint upon one portion of the wall, while Lælius assailed another. The latter was successful in forcing his way into the market-place. But the Citadel and the Temple of Æsculapius crowned the highest ground, and to reach these through barricaded streets of flat-roofed houses, six stories high, cost many days of close and deadly fighting. At last the garrison of the Citadel surrendered. Hasdrubal, with a body of deserters, who could hope for no quarter, shut themselves into the Temple, to sell their lives dearly. But the chief stole out and sought pardon from Scipio. His wife, chiding him as a coward, flung her children and then

146
B.C.

plunged herself, into the flames, which were now roaring up towards the golden roof of the fane.

As Scipio looked upon the funeral-blaze of so much glory, his heart smote him with a misgiving that Rome's day of ruin would also come at last.

The curse pronounced by Scipio on the site of Carthage rested on the desolated soil until the times of the Cæsars, when a prosperous Roman colony began to flourish on the peninsula. The greater part of the Carthaginian dominions were formed into the Roman province of Libya; while the victor, in imitation of his great predecessor and namesake, took the title of Africanus.

CHAPTER VI.

WARS IN SPAIN AND SICILY.

Treaty of Gracchus.	Numantia.
Massacre of Galba.	Roman Slaves.
Viriathus.	Servile War in Sicily.
Celtiberian War.	

THE Spain, conquered by Scipio during the Second Punic War, consisted merely of the eastern shore, with part of the basins of the Ebro and the Guadalquivir. Cato the Censor reduced the inhabitants to present submission, much as Oliver Cromwell reduced Ireland, by pitiless cruelty. But, irritated by the taxes they had to pay, and the loss of their mines of gold and silver, the Spaniards continued to struggle again and again under the Roman yoke. Most formidable of the peninsular tribes were the Lusitanians, a race of warlike shepherds, who occupied the sierras of Southern Portugal, and the Celtiberians, hardy dwellers on the plateau of Castile, even then studded, as its modern name suggests, with strong towers and castles for defence.

A gentler but more successful hand than Cato's soothed the turbulent Spaniards in 179 B.C. by a Treaty, which exacted from the people nothing except an obligation not to fortify their cities without the consent of the Romans. The author of this measure, by which Spain enjoyed an interval of rest, was Sempronius Gracchus, father of the famous revolutionists.

Peace was broken in the north of Spain by the people of Segeda beginning to rebuild their walls; in the south by the incursions of the Lusitanian shepherds. It is right to say, however, that the extortion of the Romans provoked the high-spirited natives to these breaches of the Treaty of Gracchus.

The treachery of a Roman Prætor, Sergius Galba, who induced the Lusitanians to divide into three bodies for the purpose of receiving allotments of land and then fell on them with the sword, inflicted an incurable wound upon the haughty spirit of the mountaineers. A few escaped from the massacre; among them a young shepherd named Viriathus. Becoming a guerilla chief, this daring man warred successfully for many years against the Romans in Spain, on one occasion reducing the Proconsul Servilianus to such straits in a mountain gorge that there was no resource but in acceptance of the terms offered by the gallant Lusitanian, who thus became the acknowledged ally of Rome. But Cæpio, the successor of Servilianus, broke the treaty, made war on Viriathus with the consent of the Senate, and, professing friendly intentions, bribed some friends of the chieftain to assassinate him in his tent, 140 B.C. This was the real end of the Lusitanian War, although the spirited mountaineers did not submit for a time.

Meanwhile the Celtiberians had begun a war. The strongest city in that region was Numantia, perched upon a lofty crag near the source of the Douro. From this stronghold harassing war had been often waged upon the Romans; and the chief operation undertaken by the Consuls was its siege. The story is that of Carthage repeated with slight variations: failure and disaster for years, until Scipio came to the rescue of the Roman name. Mancinus was the most egregious of the Roman blunderers. Retreating from before Numantia, he allowed himself to be cooped up in an old camp so effectually that he had to beg for the lives of his men. There was a young man in his army serving as Quæstor, whose name was dear to the Spaniards, and they refused to agree to any arrangement which had not attached to it the signature of Tiberius Gracchus.

When Mancinus was twitted at Rome with this shameful treaty, concluded without the due authority of Senate and people, he offered to give himself up to the Numantians as an expiation, while the Senate were to hold the treaty null and void. The Numantians wisely refused to receive the scape-goat of Roman treachery; and the war continued.

It was reserved, as has been said, for Scipio Africanus the Younger to bring this contest to an end. When he reached the scene of action, he found the camp in a state of utter disorganization, and set himself at once to remedy this evil. As he had done before Carthage, he drove out all persons that ministered to the vices of the army; and insisted on the use of nothing to wear or lie on except what was rigidly necessary. He set an example himself by sleeping upon straw. The season was so far spent, when rigorous drill had prepared the Roman army for action, that the general deemed it more prudent at once to form his winter camps. Ere this he had been joined by Jugurtha with a body of Numidian horse and some elephants.

Next spring he drew so close a line round the devoted city that no effort of the besieged within or their friends without could avail to break the fatal enclaspment. Famine wasted the wretched garrison, until all the sodden hides on which they fed were gone, and they were fain to fall with wolfish madness on the bodies of their slain comrades. The neighbouring town of Lubia tried to make a diversion in their favour; but Scipio forced the authorities there to surrender the friends of Numantia to him, and hewed off their right hands.

133 B.C.

The Numantians soon submitted, gnawed to the very bones with dreadful hunger. Some committed suicide rather than yield; and indeed the men, who tottered from the opened gates, were more like spectres than living beings.

North-western Spain had been previously traversed by Decius Brutus, who penetrated to the Biscay shore, and received the homage of the wild tribes dwelling in the wooded clefts of the Asturias.

An insurrection of the slaves in Sicily filled Rome at this time with great alarm. Owing to the vast conquests of the century, the market was glutted with captives; and the hillsides of every pastoral district were covered with gaunt and shaggy-locked men, who had once worn swords but were now doomed to carry the ignoble goad. Their food was scanty and of the coarsest kind—their clothing often what they could strip from the passing traveller—their lodging a great bare gloomy jail, lighted with a few narrow loopholes. It is little wonder that the slaves of Southern Italy became brigands at the first opportunity of escape they had.

At Enna, the centre of a grazing district in Sicily, the First Servile War broke out. Taking as their chief a Syrian slave named Eunus, who, by pretending to breathe fire and to tell fortunes, had acquired the reputation of a wizard, a mob of infuriated men in sheepskin, armed with sickles, spits, and burned stakes, rushed into the city of Enna, took speedy vengeance on the cruel master and mistress, who had so aggravated the wretchedness of their lot, and broke open all the slave prisons, whose inmates swelled their ranks.

Eunus, finding himself at the head of ten thousand men, assumed the name of Antiochus. He was soon joined by a reinforcement of revolted slaves from Agrigentum under Cleon.

The Prætors and Consuls were in turn defeated, until Rupilius reduced Tauromenium by famine, and then advanced upon Enna, which had hitherto resisted assault. The reduction of this stronghold put an end to the insurrection of the slaves. Eunus, who fled like a coward, was taken in a cave, and perished miserably in a dungeon at Murgantia.

After the conclusion of the war a code of regulations was framed to improve the condition of the agricultural districts; a change under which Sicily began once more to wear the aspect, which had caused it to be styled The Garden of Italy. 131 B.C.

CHAPTER VII.

THE GRACCHI.

Tiberius Gracchus.	Death of Scipio Minor.	Death of Caius
His Agrarian Law.	Caius Gracchus.	Cornelia.
Slain in the Capitol.	Sempronian Laws.	

THE Servile War was a symptom of the corruption and decay, which had begun to weaken the great Roman Republic. The public elections, at which votes began to be bought and sold, afforded evidence of the same. The State was internally convulsed by the struggles of the *Optimates* or new nobility, consisting of wealthy Plebeians as well as Patricians, and the *Populares*, who represented the mass of the people; and it needed but a very slight fanning to kindle the flame of a Revolution.

There was then, in Rome a man, aged almost forty, who had long been looking with pitiful eyes upon the condition of the yeomen and small farmers, and who had long cherished the hope of effecting a reform in their favour. His name was Tiberius Sempronius Gracchus, and he was the son of that statesman of splendid tastes, who in 179 conferred the boon of a judicious treaty upon Spain. But it was perhaps rather from Cornelia, the daughter of the elder Africanus, that Tiberius Gracchus inherited the greatness of his soul. This lady, on becoming a widow, refused the proposals of the King of Egypt, and devoted herself to the care of her three children—her daughter Sempronia, and her two sons —Tiberius, mild and grave—Caius, hot and fiery. The pride of Cornelia in her sons may be understood from her hopeful boast that she sought to be remembered, not as the daughter of Scipio, but as the mother of the Gracchi.

Tiberius served gallantly as a soldier both at Carthage and in Spain. In 134 B.C. he was elected to the Tribuneship, and entered with zeal upon his career as a reformer. Before long he proposed an Agrarian Law, based upon that of Licinius, and levelled at the

133 B.C.

rich landholders, who had monopolized the Public Lands at merely nominal rents.

The chief clauses of this Bill were :—

1. That no head of a family should hold more than 500 *jugera* of the State lands.
2. That for every grown son 250 additional *jugera* were to be allotted; but that the family estate should in no case exceed 1000 *jugera*.
3. That the surplus land was to be divided in lots of 30 *jugera*, partly among the needy burgesses, and partly among the Italian allies, to be held in lease from the State, and used for agriculture.
4. That those giving up their land should receive compensation for improvements.
5. That the distribution of the lands should be committed to three men (*Triumviri*).

When Gracchus in the Forum, paved with brown expectant faces, bade the clerk read his law, Octavius the Tribune, who had been gained over by the aristocracy, put his *veto* on the proceeding. This prevented the voting for a time. Meanwhile Gracchus sealed up the public treasure-chest, and suspended the business of the Government. Again the Assembly met, and again Octavius exercised his power of forbidding the law to be read. At the entreaty of a friend Gracchus referred the matter to the Senate; but was greeted there with cries of anger.

He then took a step at variance with the spirit of the Roman Constitution. By the vote of the Tribes he caused his opponent Octavius to be divested of his office as Tribune; and the lictors removed the deposed official from his bench. The law was then passed; Tiberius, his brother, and his wife's father being named as Triumvirs to allot the land.

Gracchus, who now went about the city with a body-guard of some thousand friends, next proposed that the riches of Attalus, King of Pergamus, which had been bequeathed to the Roman people, should be given to those about to receive the allotments, in order to enable them to stock their farms and build dwellings. Other schemes of reform were propounded by him, in view of the approaching Comitia, at which, contrary to Roman law, he intended to offer himself for reëlection to the Tribuneship.

The first divisions voted for his reëlection; then came a *veto*, which stopped proceedings for the day. That evening Gracchus, who well knew the effect of dramatic appeal on the hot Italian temperament, walked into the Forum, clad in black, and holding his little son by the hand. As if conscious that his life was in danger, he committed his boy to the care of the people. They raised an encouraging cheer, and some of them guarded his house all night.

When Tiberius appeared at the Capitol next morning, he was surrounded by a noisy and delighted crowd of adherents, amid whose crush he perceived a Senator making signs to him. From this friend he learned that the landholders, headed by Nasica, who had just made a violent speech in the Senate sitting hard by in the Temple of Fidelity, had resolved to kill him. Tiberius told those nearest in the crowd of his danger, upon which they girt their togas tightly round them, seized the halberds of the sergeants, and broke the staves up into batons of convenient size. Those on the outskirts of the crowd could not hear the Tribune's voice, so that he was obliged to telegraph his danger to them by touching his head with his hand. At once his enemies raised a cry "He seeks a crown"; and the news flashed into the Senate. Nasica, furious at the Consul for refusing to interfere, called on his supporters to follow him, and, wrapping the skirt of his robe round his head, an action which his followers imitated, made his way to the Capitol. There with clubs and legs torn from the benches the Patrician mob set upon the guards of Gracchus, knocking them down on every side. Tiberius fled towards the Temple of Jupiter; but the doors were shut. In his hurry he tripped over a dead body or a bench, and fell. Just as he was rising, a Tribune, one of his own colleagues, beat him down again with the leg of a stool; another baton fell on his broken skull; and he sank dead before the statues of the Seven Kings. Three hundred of his partisans shared his fate. Thus perished Tiberius Gracchus in the first sedition that had stained Rome with civil blood.

Caius Gracchus begged his brother's body for the purpose of burying it; but it was thrown into the Tiber.

Scipio, who came home to celebrate his Numantian Triumph, was now the foremost man in Rome. A demagogue named Carbo, stirred up the question of the Public Lands again; and Scipio incurred suspicion of having betrayed Roman interests to the Italians, whose wrongs at the hands of the Triumvirs he had undertaken to make known. He spoke in the Senate on this subject; and all Rome was preparing next morning to hear a second oration from him in the Forum, when the news spread that he had been found dead in bed, with the heads of his speech etched on the wax-coated tablet by his pillow, 129 B.C. It was suspected that Carbo had caused him to be strangled.

Some quiet years succeeded, troubled only by the fears of the Romans and the hopes of the Italians that the franchise would be soon extended to the latter. Flaccus, Consul for 125, brought in a Bill to this effect; but it was laid aside, to the dismay and anger of the Italian towns. Fregellæ took up arms in the rage of disappointment, but suffered severely for its rashness.

Meanwhile Caius Gracchus had been serving as Quæstor in Sardinia, where the Senate would gladly have kept him a third year. But he chose to come home in 124 B.C.; and, when summoned before the Censors that he might be publicly rebuked and expelled from the Senate, he silenced his enemies by his bold words.

"I have served twelve campaigns," said he, "although I needed to have served only ten. As Quæstor I attended my general three years, though the law would have allowed me to return home after one. The purse I carried with me full has come back empty; yet I know men, who carried out barrels full of wine, and brought them back full of gold and silver."

In 123 B.C. Caius Gracchus was fourth on the list at the election of Tribunes of the people. So great was the throng that flowed into the city to vote for him, that some were forced to answer from the house-tops. He shone out now in full lustre as an accomplished orator, so careful in the modulation of his voice that a slave, standing behind him with a flute, gave him the proper note on which to begin. One subject filled and coloured all his speeches—the death of his brother Tiberius; and bitterly he reproached the

Commons for permitting their champion to be slain and his sacred office degraded.

A sketch like this cannot describe all the laws he brought forward—some aimed at those concerned in the murder of his brother—others (called the Sempronian Laws) intended to improve the condition of the people or weaken the power of the Senate. The distribution of the Public Lands and the sale of corn at a low price to the poor were among the objects he strove to attain. It was owing to his desire to divide the aristocracy, that the order of *Equites*, principally consisting of wealthy merchants and entitled to wear a gold finger-ring as their badge, received distinct recognition.

Having caused the election of Fannius, an old friend of Tiberius, as one of the Consuls, to the exclusion of the Patrician Opimius, Gracchus was himself reëlected to the Tribuneship by the unanimous acclaim of the people. One of his colleagues was Fulvius Flaccus, who without delay brought forward his favourite scheme for the extension of the franchise to the Latin and Italian allies. Drusus put a *veto* on the law to the great delight of the Romans.

This young Tribune then quite eclipsed the scheme of colonization at Capua and Tarentum, framed by Gracchus, by proposing to form twelve new colonies, each of three thousand families, who should receive land, but pay no rent.

Gracchus had already fixed on Carthage as the site for a new colony, to be called Junonia. Going thither with Flaccus to allot the land, he met with omens that seemed to portend disaster. The new flag-staff was snapped by a storm, which blew the sacrifices from the altars; and wolves tore down the boundary marks of the new city. On his return, a man most hostile to him—Opimius the Patrician—was elected Consul; and the horizon seemed charged with storm. Neither Gracchus nor Flaccus had meanwhile been recalled to the Tribunes' bench.

The policy of Opimius was to repeal the laws of Gracchus, and so provoke him to some act which would justify his destruction. It was accordingly proposed amongst other things to annul the law for the colonization of Carthage.

121 B.C.

On the appointed day a lictor at the Capitol, pushing

rudely past with the entrails of the sacrifices, cried out to Gracchus, as he jostled him aside, "Make way for honest men!" The ex-Tribune looked sternly at the insolent official, and some rash hand struck a dagger into the man's breast. A heavy rain dispersed the crowd; but the body of the dead lictor was carried publicly on a bier to the Senate-house. Opimius, having received a senatorial decree, which sanctioned the destruction of Gracchus as a public enemy, summoned the Patricians and their slaves to arms. Flaccus collected a band in his house, plied them all night with wine, and next morning led them with Celtic weapons in their hands to the Aventine.

Thither too went Gracchus, in spite of his wife's clinging entreaties. He wore his toga, but had a little dagger below its folds. After some attempts on the side of Gracchus at reconciliation, the forces of Opimius advanced and discharged a shower of arrows, which had the effect of dispersing the rebels at once. Flaccus, caught hiding in a bath, was killed. Gracchus went into the Temple of Diana to kill himself, but a friend removed his dagger. He then crossed the Tiber by the Sublician Bridge, at the head of which, to cover his escape, two of his friends emulated the ancient heroism of Horatius. In a grove sacred to the Furies, a little farther on, the ex-Tribune was found dead, pierced at his own command by the sword of a faithful servant, who then slew himself. Its weight in gold had been offered for his head: a soldier named Septimuleius took out the brain, filled the cavity with lead, and carried off a large sum as the reward of his sorry trick. The body was thrown into the Tiber, whose yellow current rolled also hundreds of his partisans to the sea.

Cornelia survived her sons, of whose fate she was wont to speak calmly and proudly to the learned men who frequented her table at Misenum. Her early hope was fulfilled, when on the pedestal of the bronze statue, which was raised to her memory in the Forum, were carved the words, "Cornelia, mother of the Gracchi."

GREAT NAMES OF ROMAN LITERATURE, &c.

SECOND PERIOD.

LIVIUS ANDRONICUS, earliest Roman poet—a Greek slave set free —wrote tragedies and comedies in Latin—first play acted 240 B.C.

NÆVIUS, poet—born probably in Campania—a champion of the Plebeian cause—exiled to Utica—died there about 202 B.C.—wrote a poem on the *First Punic War*, besides plays.

PLAUTUS, comic poet—born at Sarsina in Umbria about 254 B.C.—at first an actor's and a baker's drudge—died 184 B.C.—his *Comedies* are founded on Greek originals.

ENNIUS, Poet—of Greek birth—native of Rudiæ in Calabria—born 239 B.C.—friend of the Scipios—author of an historical epic, the *Annates*, of which there are fragments.

CATO, the Censor—born at Tusculum in 234 B.C.—noted for his hatred of luxury—the great rival of Scipio Africanus the elder—died 149 B.C.—author of *De Re Rustica*, a household and rural miscellany—*Letters* to his son—and an historical work, *Origines*—of the two last we have only fragments.

TERENCE, comic poet—born at Carthage 195 B.C.—slave of a Roman Senator, who set him free—his chief patrons were Lælius and the younger Scipio—died in Greece about 159 B.C.—six of his plays remain—he acquired fame by the *Andria*.

LUCILIUS, satirist—born at Suessa of the Aurunci, 148 B.C.—died at Naples 103 B.C.—friend of Scipio and Lælius—earliest of the four great writers of Latin *Satire*.

THIRD PERIOD.

CHAPTER I.

MARIUS AND SULLA.

Jugurthine War.	First Mithridatic War.	Return of Sulla.
Teutones and Cimbri.	Flight of Marius.	The Colline Gate.
Saturninus and Drusus.	Marius in Rome.	Proscriptions.
Social War.	His death.	Puteoli.

In 111 the Jugurthine War began. When Micipsa, the son of Masinissa, died, he left his kingdom to his two sons, Hiempsal and Adherbal, and their illegitimate cousin, Jugurtha, whom he named Regent and guardian. Jugurtha murdered Hiempsal, and made war on Adherbal, who fled to Rome. Sowing gold broad-cast, Jugurtha then contrived to induce the Roman Senate to divide the kingdom so as to leave him the western and stronger half. He lost no time in besieging Cirta, his cousin's capital; and, having got possession of Adherbal, put him to death by torture.

The Romans then declared war against Jugurtha. By his golden bribes, however, Jugurtha managed to render the Roman generals very slack in their efforts; but Memmius the Tribune boldly exposed his wiles, and urged the people to continue the war. The crafty African now appeared in Rome as a suppliant; but, when news came that Massiva, grandson of Masinissa, had been murdered by his means, he received orders to depart at once from the city.

After the war had lingered for two years, the conduct of it was given to Quintus Metellus, who took with him as one of his lieutenants Caius Marius, a man of rough undaunted bearing, then verging upon fifty years of age.

Marius was born near Arpinum in 157 B.C.—the son of

a Latin yeoman. At the siege of Numantia and elsewhere he fought so bravely that when Scipio was asked one night at supper where a great general would be found when he was gone, he laid his hand on Marius' shoulder and said, "Here, perhaps." Becoming Tribune of the Plebs in 119, Marius displayed undaunted spirit in resisting the Patricians. On one occasion he forced the Senate to pass a Bill against illegal voting, by committing the Consul Metellus to prison. Under the brother of that Consul, Marius, who meanwhile had held the Prætorship and fought in Spain, went upon the Jugurthine War.

The first care of Metellus was to organize and discipline his army: this occupied the autumn of 109 B.C.

In the following year Jugurtha made a bold stand against the Romans at the River Muthul, but was defeated with the loss of many elephants. The siege of Zama then occupied the Legions until the surprise of his camp by Jugurtha, and the resistance of the place compelled Metellus to go into winter quarters.

Negotiations were opened with Jugurtha, who had even given up his elephants and deserters, and had promised to pay 200,000 pounds of silver, when a demand for the surrender of the King himself suddenly destroyed all hopes of peace.

In 107 the troops of Metellus marched inland across a desert, carrying skins full of water, to take the town of Thala, whither Jugurtha had retired with his children and his money-bags. But the King escaped, and soon found a refuge with his father-in-law, Bocchus, King of Mauretania.

Meanwhile Marius, whose constant saying in the camp was, "Give me half the army, and I will soon have Jugurtha in chains," had gone to Rome to stand for the Consulship. Metellus, sneering at his pretensions, had delayed his leave of absence as long as possible. But the people greeted him with joy, and he was elected by a vast majority of votes 107 B.C.

The next step of Marius was to obtain a vote of the Tribes transferring to himself the command of the Jugurthine army, which the Senate had decreed to Metellus until the completion of the war. Then, having made vast levies, drawn even from the lowest class on the Censor's register, he went over to Africa.

The war was virtually over, the only remaining task being to secure the person of Jugurtha. Marius, however, took Capsa in the desert, and wasted his energies on a fortress by the Molochath, in returning from which a vast body of African cavalry threatened his army with destruction, but were scattered by a surprise. They hung menacingly on his rear, until Sulla the Quæstor with his cavalry force completed their dispersion.

Sulla, who was afterwards to come into such fatal rivalry with Marius, was a bold blue-eyed guardsman of thirty-one, whose pale and pimpled face told of deep drinking and a dissolute life. He possessed the art of pleasing men, and in cavalry fighting was the Murat of the ancient world.

The capture of Jugurtha was mainly due to the daring of Sulla, who went, on peril of his life, or at least his liberty, into the camp of Bocchus to treat for the betrayal of the Numidian King. The cool diplomacy of the young Roman gained its end. Entrapped into an ambush by the wiles of his wife's father, Jugurtha was seized in the midst of the dead bodies of his guard.

Marius did not much relish the claims of Sulla to the sole honour of this capture. The captive King walked in chains before the chariot of the triumphant Consul. The mob rent his clothes off, and twitched the jewels from his bleeding ears. "What a bath of ice!" exclaimed the African, as they thrust him into the old underground cell at the Capitol to starve to death, 104 B.C.

Gauda, his puny and imbecile half-brother, was then made King of Numidia, which however was much diminished in size by an addition to Mauretania.

Meanwhile a terrible cloud, growing blacker every year, had been hanging over the northern frontier of the Roman dominions. A vast multitude of barbarians, principally consisting of the Cimbri and Teutones, tribes of the Germanic race, came pouring from the north; and one Roman general after another had been learning by defeat to dread the red glitter of their copper helmets, and the sweeping whirl of their long swords. From 113 B.C., when the home-

less Cimbri first defeated Carbo in Carinthia, down to 105
B.C., when disaster culminated in the defeat of Maximus
and Cæpio at Arausio (*Orange*) on the Rhone—a defeat
which cost Rome eighty thousand soldiers—blow after blow
fell upon the dismayed legionaries. In this crisis all eyes
turned to Marius. He was still in Africa with the army;
but in his absence, in spite of the law against reëlection to
the Consulship, he was made Consul for the second time,
and that distinction was afterwards conferred upon him for
five successive years (104–100). The expedition of the
Cimbri to Spain, where they met their match in the Celtiberians, delayed their invasion of Italy for a while. But in
102 B.C. the movement, so much dreaded at Rome, began.
In two divisions the barbarians prepared to enter Italy.
The Teutones and Ambrones moved down the Rhone to
gain the sea-coast road. Marius lay in an intrenched camp
at the junction of the Isère and Rhone. In vain they flung
themselves upon his works. Giving up the useless enterprise, they marched past, jibing at the Romans as they
went. Marius followed. At the wells of Aquæ Sextiæ (*Aix*)
the light troops of his army came into collision with the
Ambrones. A conflict ensued, closing with the defeat of the

**102
B.C.**
latter. Next day a great battle took place. Till
noon the Romans and Teutones stood locked in
mortal struggle; until the scorching sun wearied
the latter, and a stratagem, similar to that which
won Bannockburn—the rush of some camp-followers from
an ambuscade—decided the day for Rome. The grapes of
Aix were very plentiful and luscious for many an autumn
after that bloody day.

Meanwhile Catulus waited on the Adige for the Cimbri,
who were expected by the Tyrol. Early in 101 B.C. they
came, descending the glaciers of the Brenner Pass on their
shields. The Romans gave way for a time, but rallied on
the Po. Marius came to the aid of Catulus, and the battle
took place on the Raudian Plain below Vercellæ.

**101
B.C.**
The front lines of the Cimbrian phalanx had a
chain passed through every belt to keep the array
unbroken. But the heat of an Italian sky and the
deadly rain of Roman javelins weakened and disordered

the barbarians. They were driven back upon the waggons that walled in their camp, where their wives stood shrieking and hurling stones. The slaughter was dreadful; many of the savage women strangled themselves with their own hair. All fear of the northern invasion was dissipated by these two great victories.

Out of the necessities of this war grew a second insurrection of the slaves in Sicily, who rose in discontent because the Roman Prætor suspended the action of a senatorial decree giving freedom to those unduly kept in slavery. The story is like that of the First Servile War. A soothsayer named Salvius headed the insurrection in the east of Sicily. He failed in the siege of Murgantia. A fortune-teller named Athenio headed a rising in the west of the island, and failed to take Lilybæum. Salvius assumed regal state and the name Tryphon. Athenio succeeded him as chieftain of the slaves. The Consul Aquillius crushed the rebellion; and a number of the slaves, brought as gladiators to fight in the arena, slew one another at the foot of the altars, until one man, being left, fell upon his sword. The war lasted for three years (103 B.C.—101 B.C.)

Rome was now troubled by the combination with Marius of two demagogues, the impudent witty Glaucia and the fiery Saturninus. The three secured their election in 100 B.C.—Marius as Consul, Glaucia as Prætor, Saturninus as Tribune of the Plebs. The last-named introduced an Agrarian Law to divide the lands in Gaul, lately held by the Cimbri, among the soldiers of Marius; and, by the aid of the veterans, forcibly carried the measure in spite of senatorial opposition. Metellus, an opponent of this measure, was forced into exile; Saturninus murdered his leading antagonists. But the beating to death of Memmius, candidate against Glaucia for the Consulship, roused a furious flame of rage against Saturninus. Marius led a force against his late accomplice, who fled to the Capitol with Glaucia and others. The cutting of the water-pipes reduced the insurgents to the necessity of surrender; and some young nobles, climbing on the roof of the temporary prison, tore off the tiles, and hurled them down with fatal aim on the wretches beneath (100 B.C.).

A Tribune named Livius Drusus, attempting a reform of the State, proposed in 91 B.C. certain measures called the Livian Laws. They related to the functions of jurymen, the planting of colonies, the distribution of grain, and, most important of all, the extension of the franchise to the Italian allies. After a sharp struggle with the Roman capitalists, the laws were annulled, and their author was struck down by the hand of an assassin one evening in the twilight at his own door. His death, uprooting the hopes of the Italians, caused the outbreak of a fierce and desolating struggle, known in Roman history as the Social or Marsic War (90-88 B.C.).

The war began by a massacre of Romans at Asculum in Picenum. The warlike Marsians took the lead in the hostile movement, which soon overspread all Central and Southern Italy.

Corfinium in the Pelignian territory was selected to be the capital of the new Italian Republic. Two Consuls were elected, each with six Prætors. Coins were struck in silver with legends, alternately in the Latin and the Samnite tongue, some of them bearing an impression of the Sabellian ox struggling with the Roman she-wolf.

The first campaign was decidedly unfavourable to Rome. Campania was overrun by the revolted tribes; and the Marsian Consul Silo signally defeated the Roman Consul Lupus on the Tolenus. Marius, who was acting as Legate under the Consul, saw dead bodies floating down the stream, and came too late to the rescue.

At the beginning of the second year the Romans had the wisdom to pass the Julian Law, extending the franchise to such allies as had not appeared in arms or were now inclined to lay them down. This had the effect of tranquillizing Etruria and Umbria, then simmering into incipient rebellion; but some of the allies it hardened into more resolute defiance. Latin was now disused on the Confederate coinage, on which appeared only legends in the old Oscan tongue.

But the second campaign turned the tide of war. By the death of the Consul Cato his lieutenant Sulla received the command in Campania, whence he drove the enemy. The

Consul Pompeius took Corfinium, upon which the revolt centred in Bovianum, a fortress of the Pentrian Samnites. The betrayal of this place to Sulla, and the surrender of Asculum brought the war to a close. The allies had been well officered during the war. One of their generals Judacilius committed suicide with much ceremony at Asculum before its surrender. After supping with his friends he left the hall, drank a goblet of poisoned wine, and ascended a pyre, to which his guests applied torches.

Arrangements were now made for admitting to the Latin franchise even communities between the Po and the Alps; but this concession was qualified. The Samnites still remained in arms; although the Social War was over.

During the Social War the allies had sent an embassy seeking aid from Mithridates VI., King of Pontus, and had received a promise of help. This monarch, a learned and clever man, being irritated at the loss of Phrygia, which the Romans had given to his father but had lately taken back, interfered in the affairs of Cappadocia and Bithynia, and established himself in Pergamus as the deliverer of Asia Minor from the Roman yoke. The Romans declared war against him, and appointed Sulla to the command; a proceeding which gave bitter offence to Marius, now growing old and fat.

Aided by the Tribune Sulpicius, who caused the Italians to be distributed among the tribes, and made all freedmen who had served in the Italian Wars equal with the old citizens, Marius managed to have the command transferred from Sulla to himself.

Sulla, hurrying to Nola, found himself already ousted from command, upon which he made a speech to his soldiers that kindled them into furious action. They stoned the officers of Marius, and demanded to be led to Rome. In conjunction with the Consul Pompeius, Sulla advanced, and, seizing the approaches to the city, entered it with two legions. A furious conflict in the streets resulted in the victory of Sulla and the flight of Marius, who with eleven others was pronounced a traitor. Sulpicius, one of the eleven, was arrested and killed.

The adventures of Marius were manifold. Sailing from

Ostia, he was driven by a storm to land at Circeii. After plodding along the shore for two weary days, and hiding in a forest to escape the cavalry who were scouring the country, he caught sight of two ships, and plunged into the sea to swim out to one of them. The horsemen galloped down to the beach, and shouted to the captain to yield up Marius, who, wet and exhausted, pleaded with tears to be retained. The captain kept him for the time, but soon, landing him at the Liris on pretence of having to wait for the land wind, put out to sea, leaving him alone. A herdsman hid him among the reeds; but the approach of some horsemen, who asked about him, frightened him so much that he plunged into the river, whence he was dragged all wet and muddy to the jail of Minturnæ. After some hesitation it was resolved by the town council to obey Sulla and kill the great captive. A Celtic slave was sent, sword in hand, into the dark cell to do the deed; but the fiery eyes of the old lion crouching in the corner, and the thunderous growl of his question, "Darest thou slay Cáius Marius?" so frightened or touched the man that he flung the weapon down and fled. The magistrates then permitted Marius to escape. He got on board a ship and landed near Carthage. The Prætor sent a messenger requiring him to leave the province at once; and, when the quailing officer, fixed by a glare of the imperial eye, asked what answer he should return, the veteran replied, " Tell him that you saw Caius Marius sitting among the ruins of Carthage." Marius and his son afterwards obtained leave to remain in Africa.

Sulla went to Greece in 87 B.C. for the purpose of opposing Archelaus, the general of Mithridates, who had occupied Athens. After a tedious siege the Roman general made himself master of Athens and the Piræus (86 B.C.); but sullied his laurels by committing to the flames the grand old buildings and monuments of the historic city. He then defeated the Pontic armies in the battles of Chæronea and Orchomenus.

Meanwhile at Rome the Old and the New Citizens continued their contentions. The Consul Cinna, heading the latter faction, was stripped of his authority and expelled from the city by the Senate. He went to Nola, where he managed to secure in his favour not only a part of Sulla's army, discontented at not being taken to the Eastern War, but also the Samnite garrison of the place. Many of the Italian cities also declared for him. He entered into correspondence with Marius, who came to Etruria and accepted service under his banner. The united armies, surrounding Rome, forced the trembling Senate to invite them into the city, which Marius entered with ragged unkempt beard and hair, and an ominous frown upon his brow.

For many days Rome ran red with slaughter. Any man, who passed Marius without a low obeisance, was slain on the spot. The gory head of an orator, who had formerly spoken against the general, was brought in a charger to his supper-table. The dagger paid many a grudge and cancelled many a debt during that week of terror in Rome; and the slaves ran riot with the treasures of their murdered masters. It was not until Sertorius, an officer of Cinna, began to slay the butchers with the edge of the sword, that the wholesale murdering abated. Sulla's house was thrown down; and his name branded as that of a traitor.

87 B.C.

When the time came round, Marius without any election assumed the Consulship in company with Cinna. It was the seventh time for the peasant of Arpinum. Thirteen days later, drunk with blood and wine, he laid down the life he had latterly so terribly abused (86 B.C.).

Before the victory of Sulla at Orchomenus the Marian party had sent Flaccus into Greece to supersede him in the conduct of the Mithridatic War. This general, however, was murdered near the Hellespont by his own Legate, Fimbria, who then made war on Mithridates. Sulla now saw the importance of concluding a peace with the Pontic King, with whom he held a favourable conference in the Troad. The terms agreed to were that Mithridates should resume his old position, abandoning all his conquests, paying the costs of the war, and giving up his ships (84 B.C.). Sulla then blockaded Fimbria in Thyatira. The desertion of his soldiers left the adventurer helpless; he fled to Pergamus and killed himself.

Sulla enriched his soldiers with wealth extorted from

Asia Minor, before he sailed from Ephesus to Athens. Thence he took the valuable library of Apellicon. Marching overland to Patræ on the other side of Greece, he embarked his troops there, and landed at Brundusium in Italy early in 83 B.C.

Meanwhile the Consuls Carbo and Cinna had been making great preparations to oppose him. A force of two hundred thousand was gathered for the war; and some divisions were shipped across to Dalmatia. But in a mutiny that broke out at Ancona Cinna was killed by the blow of a stone; and Carbo then gave up the idea of a contest in Greece.

Sulla's army consisted at first of only forty thousand men, but he was joined by several persons of note, among whom were two young men named Pompey and Crassus. We shall hear of them again.

83 B.C.

Giving strict orders to his soldiers to injure the property of the Italians in no way, Sulla marched over the Apennines into Campania. There he defeated the Consul Norbanus at Capua; and at Teanum by bribery and soft words tricked Scipio out of an army, which joined his banner in a mass. Sertorius, the Legate, who had warned Scipio against the foxy wiles of Sulla, escaped into Spain. Then came the winter, during which both sides braced their strength for a final struggle.

Carbo and young Marius were the new Consuls. The latter, defying Sulla to fight, lost the battle of Sacriportus by the desertion of some cohorts, and was obliged to shut himself up in Præneste, leaving the way open to Rome. A secret message, which he sent to the Prætor of the city, caused the massacre of Sulla's adherents in the Senate.

82 B.C.

Leaving an officer to besiege Præneste, Sulla then proceeded to Rome; but almost immediately afterwards went up the Clanis to attack the camp of Carbo in Etruria. While engaged in this enterprise, he heard that an army of Samnites and Lucanians under two brave princes was on the march from the mountains to relieve Præneste. Then began a race, which Sulla won. When the mountaineers reached the passes leading to the city of their destination, they found the soldiers of Sulla guarding all the approaches and covering Præneste. And so for a while the armies waited, like tigers crouched for a spring.

The success of Metellus at Placentia in the valley of the Po, and other disasters so disheartened Carbo that he fled to Africa. The fragments of his army effected a junction with the Samnites and Lucanians, and the united forces marched to Rome by the Latin Road, and came in the evening to the Colline Gate. It was a night of terrible suspense in Rome. Pontius at dawn assured his men that the Roman wolf had now been tracked home to its lair, and would soon be deprived of all power to harm. Then the allies assailed the gate and walls. Before long the helmets of approaching horsemen were seen glittering from a cloud of dust. It was Sulla's vanguard. By noon his whole army had arrived, and in spite of their weariness the conflict began at once. Conspicuous on a white horse, Sulla, in person led the left wing against the Samnites, while the right under Crassus assailed Carbo's men. The victory of the latter was easy and complete; Sulla held his own against the Samnites, but when night fell he had been driven back against the wall. Joining Crassus in the darkness, he continued the struggle next day, and won a decisive victory. Among the fifty thousand slain was Pontius the Samnite chief. Sulla met the assembled Senate in the Temple of Bellona, and, as business was beginning, from the neighbouring Circus there arose the rattle of armour and cries of pain. Some of the Senate started up in dismay; but Sulla coolly cried, "Sit down. It is only a few wretches undergoing the punishment they deserve." The few wretches numbered six thousand of the Samnite race, who were butchered in cold blood (82 B.C.).

Young Marius, seeing the surrender of Præneste inevitable, attempted to escape by a subterranean passage in company with the brother of Pontius. They found the entrance blocked up, and agreed to kill each other. Marius, being only wounded at first, induced a slave to give him a mortal stab.

The Second Mithridatic War forms a small episode of the

time (83-81 B.C.). The Pontic King refused to restore Cappadocia, as agreed upon in the treaty. Murena, the Roman lieutenant, instigated by Archelaus, now a deserter, invaded that kingdom, but was defeated by Mithridates at Sinope. Peace was soon afterwards made.

The massacre of Marius was kind and gentle compared with the Proscriptions of Sulla. Lists of doomed men were published from day to day; and two talents were paid to the slayer of any one whose name was written therein. Men, who wished another slain, had his name inserted. Slaves slew their masters; sons, their fathers; wives got their husbands proscribed. The porch of Sulla's house was full of gory heads. Foremost among the human fiends of this dreadful time was Catiline the Conspirator. In those parts of Italy, which had taken up arms for Marius, the same bloody business was done

Assuming for an indefinite time the title and state of Dictator—an office disused since the Second Punic War—Sulla proceeded to shape the Roman Constitution after his own tastes. He rewarded the army to which he owed his position by allotments in different parts of Italy, where lands had been confiscated. To ten thousand slaves he gave the Roman franchise, in order to surround himself with a devoted body-guard. These called themselves the Cornelii. Space will not permit us to detail his reforms, which aimed at the restoration of the ancient Constitution. His Criminal Code was a success; his Political Reforms were for the most part unavailing.

In 80 B.C. Sulla laid down the Dictatorship, and retired to his villa at Puteoli. There, often floating over the sapphire waters of the beautiful bay, hunting in the chestnut glades, or jesting and singing with a rose-garland on his brow and a wine-cup in his hand, he spent the last two years of his life in ease or sensuality. The task of composing *Memorials of his Time* in Greek, gave occupation to his evenings; and he was engaged on this work two days before his death. The rupture of a blood-vessel carried him off in his sixtieth year, (78 B.C.).

CHAPTER II.

POMPEY AND CÆSAR.

Sertorian War.	Catiline and Cicero.	Pharsalia.
Spartacus.	First Triumvirate.	Murder of Pompey.
The Cilician Pirates.	Cæsar in Gaul.	Thapsus and Munda.
Third Mithridatic War.	The Rubicon.	Murder of Cæsar.

POMPEY, son of the avaricious Strabo, whose death by lightning pleased everybody, was born in 106 B.C. We have already seen him levying troops in Picenum and joining the banner of Sulla, to whom he rendered the greatest service. Before the death of the Dictator this gallant youth was sent to Sicily, where Carbo was at the head of a fragment of the Marian party. Pompey defeated and slew Carbo, after which he received orders to carry the war into Africa against Domitius Ahenobarbus (Brassbeard). He had some difficulty in getting his troops away from Carthage, where they all began to dig for buried gold among the ruins; but in the short space of forty days he succeeded in defeating Brassbeard, and got besides some noble sport among the lions and elephants of the region. When Sulla saw this young man of twenty-four the idol of his soldiers, he prudently greeted him with the title of *Magnus;* and, though unwilling at first to adopt so unusual a course, allowed him to enjoy the honour of a Triumph, although he had not reached senatorial rank.

After Sulla's death the Consul Lepidus, aiming at supreme power, raised an army in Transalpine Gaul and marched to Rome. His colleague Catulus, and his former supporter Pompey defeated him at the Milvian Bridge; but his lieutenant Brutus held out long in Mutina (*Modena*). Him however Pompey afterwards subdued and put to death.

The brave Sertorius had meanwhile gallantly maintained the Marian cause in Spain. His wisdom and kindness won the favour of the Spaniards, whose superstitious feelings were also touched, when they saw a tame white doe always at his heels. Organizing a Senate of three hundred, partly Roman, partly Spanish, and establishing at Osca (*Huesca*) a school in which Spanish boys were taught Greek and Latin, he made his party so strong in Spain, that the new western republic bore all the assaults of Metellus Pius the Roman general. Pompey sought and obtained from the Senate the command in Spain as Proconsul. The success of Sertorius continued. He took Lauron: Pompey defeated his lieutenants near Valencia. On the Sucro they came face to face; and it was the approach of Metellus that saved Pompey. "Ah," cried sarcastic Sertorius, "what a whipping I should have given the boy, if the old lady had not come up!" The difficulty of meeting a guerilla force, which melted before attack to reünite unexpectedly in a new place, prolonged the war. Sertorius concluded a treaty with Mithridates, in order that Rome might be assailed both on the east and the west; but his assassination in 72 B.C., at Osca at the supper-table of Perperna, one of the lieutenants of Lepidus who had joined him, changed the aspect of affairs. Perperna, who took the chief command, was easily defeated, and slain by Pompey.

In 73 B.C. Spartacus, a Thracian gladiator, making his escape from the school of Capua, made a stand on Mount Vesuvius, where he was joined by so many gladiators and slaves that he was able to defeat the Roman Prætors. He then went ravaging through Picenum into Cisalpine Gaul and back to the very extremity of the southern peninsula; where he besieged Rhegium in the hope of getting over to Sicily, the nest of all Servile Wars. He paid some pirates to ferry his army across, but they took the money and sailed away. Crassus, to whom the war was intrusted, drew a line across the upper part of Calabria,

71 B.C. for the purpose of confining Spartacus to the foot of the Italian boot; but the gladiator broke through, and darted on Brundusium in the hope of seizing ships. Baffled there by the presence of a Roman force, he turned back to fight with Crassus, who was pursuing him. A terrible struggle ensued, in which Spartacus was defeated and slain (71 B.C.). The victor strung up the bodies of his captives to the number of six thousand along the road from Rome to Capua. Pompey, returning from Spain, intercepted a body of fugitives in the north of Italy, and put them all to the sword; an achievement which led him to claim the honour of having "cut up the war by the roots."

Pompey and Crassus obtained the Consulship in the year 70 B.C., mainly owing to the trained armies they kept together. One of Pompey's principal achievements in politics during the year was the restoration to the Tribunes of that power which Sulla had taken from them.

The Mediterranean was at that time infested with swarms of pirates, who, encouraged by Mithridates, the Pontic King, made descents upon the Italian shores in galleys, often gleaming with purple and gold. So daring had they become that they descended even upon Ostia, and were wont to plunder the villas and seize the wealthy Romans on the roads not far from the Capitol. Roman commerce was for the time paralyzed. In 67 B.C. Gabinius proposed that the task of attacking these pirates should be intrusted to a consular person. Pompey was meant by this phrase; and to him the command was given. Dividing the Mediterranean into thirteen districts, and spreading the fleet over these, he swept the sea as with a net, driving the pirates before him towards their chief nest in Cilicia, where they held the gorges of Taurus. In forty days the western sea was clear. Then, brushing the wasps out of every inlet in Greece and her islands, he collected the whole swarm at Coracesium on the Cilician coast, and crushed them at a blow. This complete success was achieved in three months.

The Third Mithridatic War, kindled partly by the embassies of Sertorius, had meanwhile been raging since 74 B.C. The King of Bithynia having left his dominions to the Romans by a will, the Pontic monarch interfered, invaded, and took the country. Mithridates then laid siege to Cyzicus. Lucullus, being appointed to an Asiatic command, so hemmed him in and straitened his supplies there, that his army broke into pieces and fled towards Lampsacus. Step by step Lucullus then drove Mithridates before him, until Sinope the Pontic capital fell; and at the end of the third campaign all Pontus was in the hands of the Romans, and its King was a fugitive with his son-in-law, Tigranes, in Armenia. Lucullus then proceeded to regulate the affairs of Asia, a task which he performed mildly and with justice.

Upon the refusal of Tigranes in 69 B.C. to give up Mithridates, the Roman general invaded Armenia; and Tigranes, pulling the crown from his head, was soon forced by a complete defeat to abandon his capital. He was defeated again in the following year. But mutiny among the Roman troops, fomented by Clodius, afterwards the foe of Cicero, paralyzed the efforts of Lucullus, upon which Mithridates made a dash upon Pontus and defeated the Roman officer in command there.

Affairs were in this state, when the Manilian Law, eloquently supported by Cicero, conferred on Pompey the Asiatic command, with powers equal to those of a Dictator. The meeting between Lucullus and his successor was stormy. Pompey then defeated Mithridates near the Euphrates by the light of a dim moon. Tigranes would give no more aid, so that the Pontic King pushed towards the Caucasus and into the Crimea, where he made his last stand, threatening to pass through Scythia and descend on Italy from the north-east. Meanwhile Pompey, having founded Nicopolis on the site of his victory, marched towards the Caucasus. Swarms of venomous serpents turned him from the Caspian. Gifts and homage from the native princes came pouring in on all sides. The revolt of his son having reduced Mithridates to utter despair, he closed his career by a draught of poison 63 B.C.

Before this event Pompey went to Syria, which he made a Roman province. The siege of Jerusalem, undertaken in behoof of Hyrcanus, who disputed the Judean throne with Aristobulus, cost him three months. After the capture of the city he was irreverent enough to enter the Holy of Holies in the Temple; but there was nothing to gratify his curiosity in the place; and we can easily imagine the puzzled face of the Pagan, or rather Infidel, as all educated Romans in his day were, who held no clue to the spiritual meaning of the Jewish worship. The news of Mithridates' death recalled Pompey from Arabia to Sinope, where the funeral rites were performed. The settlement of his conquests in Asia, a task which he accomplished *without* the authority of the Senate, then occupied Pompey for some time, after which he made his way slowly homeward, arriving in 61 B.C., after more than six years of absence. The sums he brought to the Roman treasury by his victories were enormous ; and his two days' Triumph was of surpassing splendour. It was the third he had enjoyed; and he could now boast of having triumphed over the whole world, as then known, for his first had been over Africa, his second for victories in Europe, while the last and greatest commemorated his achievements in Asia.

Two other great names had for some time been mingling themselves prominently with Roman history.

Caius Julius Cæsar, a Patrician of the Julian gens, was born in 100 B.C. The marriage of his aunt to Marius connected him closely with the party of that great soldier ; and the connection was strengthened by his own union with Cornelia, daughter of Cinna, the leader of the Marian party after the death of its chief. The keen-eyed Sulla saw in the youth, as he expressed it, "many Mariuses." Cæsar was a man of cultivated mind; his oratory, in which he shone during the impeachment of Dolabella for extortion in Macedonia, was moulded partly by the instructions of Apollonius Molo, whose lectures he attended at Rhodes. In his desire for popularity Cæsar spent great sums of money, in fact got deeply into debt; but from this his Spanish campaigns set him free. Quæstor in 68, Ædile in 65, Pontifex Maximus in 63,—in all offices he displayed the same great genius and lavish generosity.

Marcus Tullius Cicero was six years older, having been born at Arpinum in 106 B.C. Archias of Antioch, Phædrus, Philo, and Molo were among the instructors who prepared this great orator for his forensic triumphs. The earliest of his speeches, now extant, was made in 81 B.C. After studying at Athens for a time, and acting as Quæstor in Sicily, he achieved a great success by conducting the impeachment of Verres for oppression in that island. His speech in favour of the Manilian Law has been already mentioned. In 63 B.C., although what the Romans called "a new man" (that is, one whose ancestors had not been curule magistrates), he obtained the Consulship; and for his promptitude in crushing the plot, noticed in the succeeding paragraphs, was honoured with the name, " Father of his Country."

In the bloody proscriptions of Sulla no adherent of that name was more conspicuous than Lucius Sergius Catiline. Profligate in his life, and deeply laden with debt, this poor scion of a Patrician house saw, in the troubles of a revolution, the only hope of holding his own or advancing to a higher station. His frank manners enabled him to attract the young nobles and restless veterans of Sulla's disbanded army. Having been defeated as a candidate for the Consulship of 66, owing to an impeachment which Clodius brought against him for extortion in Africa, he formed a plot to murder the two Consuls; but he gave the signal too soon, and it failed. His wicked brain then hatched a more extensive conspiracy, which came to a head during the Consulship of Cicero. The murder of Cicero, and the firing of Rome in twelve places at once were parts of his plan. But Fulvia, the mistress of one of the conspirators, informed Cicero of the plot, upon which he obtained a senatorial decree investing the Consuls with the powers of a Dictator. The Senate being convened in the Temple of Jupiter Stator, Catiline had the hardihood to enter the assembly; but every Senator shrank from him, as from a plague-struck wretch. Cicero then thundered forth an oration, at the close of which Catiline rose to reply. But a roar of anger drove him from the Senate, and in terror of his life he fled from Rome.

63
B.C.

Lentulus, Prætor of the city, and Cethegus remained to carry on the plot. A lucky chance threw evidence against them into Cicero's hands. There were then in Rome certain ambassadors of the Allobroges, a Gallic tribe between the Rhone and the Isère, who had come to entreat the remission of some debts. The coldness of their reception having made them angry, Lentulus began to tamper with them. They told their Roman patron Fabius, who told Cicero. The Consul desired them to ask for letters signed by the chief conspirators, which might satisfy their nation that the plot was real; and, when they had got these, and were just leaving Rome, they were arrested with all their writings and effects. This artful stroke extorted a confession from the conspirators, who after some deliberation were strangled in the dungeon called Tullianum.

Catiline had meanwhile collected two legions; but the news of the executions at Rome caused many to desert. With the rest he endeavoured to reach Cisalpine Gaul; but Metellus Celer had occupied the passes, and Antony, once a friend of the arch-conspirator, was following fast. He stood at bay at Pistoreia. Antony pretended to be sick, so that Petreius led the army against him. A complete defeat of the conspirators took place, and Catiline fell in the thickest of the fight. No prisoners were made, for none would yield alive.

After Cæsar came from Spain, he contrived to reconcile Pompey and Crassus, and by their support obtained the Consulship, having sacrificed his Triumph to attain that object. The union of the three—Pompey, Crassus, and Cæsar —at this time is usually called the First Triumvirate; but the secrecy of the arrangement prevents it from deserving that name. Cato the Stoic, great grandson of the Censor, was the chief opponent of the three. In spite of this rival Cæsar carried an Agrarian Law, for the purpose of rewarding Pompey's veterans with land.

59 B.C.

The Vatinian Law now appointed Cæsar, with the rank of Proconsul, to the government of Cisalpine Gaul and Illyria for *five* years. The Senate with malicious kindness added Transalpine Gaul to his provinces, hoping in their hearts for his defeat. But he did not depart immediately. Pompey's marriage to Julia, Cæsar's daughter, aided much to strengthen the union between the two men.

Clodius, whose mutiny had so thwarted Lucullus, had incurred public odium by entering Cæsar's house in the disguise of a singing girl during the mysteries of the Bona Dea. When brought to trial, he tried to escape by proving an *alibi;* but Cicero overturned his plea. In consequence of this Clodius, when Cæsar sought the removal of Cicero from Rome, readily became the instrument. It required a law to make Clodius a Plebeian that he might hold the Tribuneship; and such a law was passed. Clodius then brought in a Bill to the effect, that any magistrate, who had put Roman citizens to death without trial, should be sent into exile. This was levelled at Cicero's treatment of the conspirators who had been in league with Catiline. In vain the great orator assumed mourning, canvassed the Senate, and tried to touch Pompey's heart. A second Bill ordered him to live at least four hundred miles from Rome, and commanded the destruction of his villas. With much sorrow he left Rome, and went to Thessalonica.

The removal of Cato was managed in a different way, by sending him as Prætor to Cyprus in order to annex that island as a new province to the Roman Empire. Thus the Senate was left leaderless; and the unworthy Clodius did almost as he pleased.

Cæsar's first campaign in Gaul (58 B.C.) was signalized by a great victory over the Helvetians near Bibracté (*Autun*), and a yet greater over Ariovistus and his brave Suevi in the neighbourhood of Bâle. In facing these huge barbarians he was obliged to stimulate the flagging courage of his men by declaring that, if they did not like to fight, he would go out to battle with the Tenth Legion alone.

The chief operation of the second campaign (57 B.C.) was directed against the Nervii, most powerful of the Belgic tribes which had banded together to resist his march. They dwelt in thick woods, and took advantage of their knowledge of the country to fall upon him as he was intrenching his camp. Nothing but the energy of a Cæsar could have saved the Roman army, which was completely hemmed in. Snatching a buckler from a private soldier in the great crisis of the fight, he rushed alone on the barbarians—the gallant Tenth came to his rescue—and the tide of battle turned. This victory gave him the command of all the country between the Rhine and the sea.

In Cæsar's third campaign (56 B.C.) he subdued the shores of Brittany by means of a fleet, and reduced the warlike tribes between the Seine and the Rhine. During these distant expeditions he did not cease his intrigues at Rome. Fixing his winter residence at Lucca, he managed still to pull the wires of metropolitan politics, receiving in his quarters visits from senators and magistrates by the hundred.

A quarrel between Pompey and Clodius resulted in the recall of Cicero. In vain Clodius, now no longer Tribune, got his friends to *veto* the law: in vain he led a riotous mob for three days through the streets of Rome, burning and slaying as he went. A wild young noble named Milo collected a band of gladiators, and with their aid put down the sedition at the point of the sword. Cicero was borne back through streets crowded with citizens in holiday dress; and he was none the less welcome to the poorer classes for the fall in the price of bread, which occurred just after his return. The orator attempted to revenge himself by prosecuting Clodius for sedition; but Cato, now home from Cyprus, interfered to defend the demagogue.

In the autumn of 56 B.C. Pompey and Crassus went to Lucca to hold a conference with Cæsar. The results were the assumption by the two former of the Consulship for the ensuing year, and a new assignment of provinces among the three. Pompey received Spain; Crassus, Syria; and Cæsar was confirmed in his government of Gaul for five years more, after the expiration of his original term; that is, from 53 B.C. to 49 B.C.

In 55 B.C. Cæsar all but extirpated by wholesale slaughter two German nations, which had crossed the Rhine to attack him, and, making a bridge over the stream near Coblenz, marched into Germany with sword and flame. On his return he broke the bridge down. Taking advantage of the fact that Cæsar had been engaged in some negotiations with the Germans, when the massacre took place, Cato proposed in the Senate that this violator of faith should be delivered over to the vengeance of the barbarians. In 55 B.C. the great Roman soldier paid his first short visit to Britain, and learned to respect the warriors of Kent. Next year occurred his second and greater invasion of the island.

The news that his daughter Julia, Pompey's young wife, was dead, reached him in Gaul. Henceforth these great men, now severed by the parting of a family tie, drifted fast asunder.

The death of Crassus in the far East completed the rupture of the Triumvirate. Allured by the gold and jewels of Syria, this man, whom no abundance of wealth could satisfy, went in person to his province. A great Parthian empire had sprung up round its centre Seleucia on the Tigris; and against this his expedition was directed. The strength of these Asiatics lay in their clouds of light-armed cavalry, trained to scatter before a charge and shoot back showers of arrows at the pursuers, before whom they seemed to flee. Such a force surrounded the legions of Crassus on the scorching plains of Mesopotamia. He was defeated, but made good his retreat to the foot of the mountains. There, enticed to a conference, he was murdered; and when his head was sent to the Parthian court, King Orodes, in mockery of his avarice, bade melted gold be poured between the cold lips. The gallant son of Crassus, a brave assistant of Cæsar in the Gallic War, died in the battle. Cassius saved a division of the broken army; and for two years continued to repel the Parthians.

During the winter of 54–53, while Cæsar's army lay scattered in winter-quarters, and the general himself was, as usual, going to Northern Italy, a German chieftain, Ambiorix, attacked one of the camps and cut off two legions. A movement upon another camp was baffled by the rapid approach of Cæsar, who was so much afraid of a general rising that he borrowed a legion from Pompey. Ambiorix was defeated in the following year. But the Gallic War then broke out into a much greater blaze. Under their chief, Vercingetorix, the Arverni became the centre of a great league, resolved to free Gaul from the invader; and in the towns, all barricaded and made strong, the patriotic savages made a gallant stand. In vain. From one refuge to another the chieftain was driven to Alesia, where he ultimately surrendered (52 B.C.). Here Cæsar lay in peril between a beleaguering host, and a multitude within the town, against whom he had to draw double lines of defence round his camp. But he defeated the force outside, and then the town yielded. His campaigns against the Belgæ succeeded; and about 50 B.C. his great work of conquest was done.

Pompey did not go to Spain; but, pretending that his office as Keeper of the Corn-market required his presence at Rome, he left the management of affairs there to his lieutenants. The murder of Clodius, the popular leader, by

Milo, a senatorial chief, who met him travelling on the Appian Way, excited a dreadful riot at Rome. Pompey was appointed to restore order. Cicero, the orator, had written a speech in defence of Milo; but the appearance of Pompey's soldiers in the court frightened him into silence. Milo, being condemned, fled to Marseilles, while Pompey remained in sole command of Rome, though not dignified, as he had hoped to be, with the title of Dictator.

Cæsar, perhaps by means of Gallic gold, secured the aid of Curio, one of the noble desperadoes of the age, who gained the Tribuneship in 50 B.C. Another of his partisans was the young Mark Antony, who had latterly been acting as his Quæstor in Gaul, and who was elected a Tribune in 49 B.C.

All through the year 50 the storm-clouds grew darker. Pompey, for the purpose of weakening his rival, suggested that he should furnish a legion for the Parthian War, and also demanded the return of the legion himself had lent. Both of these legions were placed at Capua. Curio having proposed that the two generals should disband their armies, a letter came from Cæsar to the Senate, offering to resign his command, if Pompey would do the same. A hot debate ensued, resulting in the outlawry of Cæsar, and the passing of a law to invest the Consuls with the powers of a Dictator. Both Consuls were friends of Pompey.

The advantage seemed to be distinctly on Pompey's side. Cæsar, who was at Ravenna, had just one legion; while Pompey, in addition to the three he had collected, believed, as he boastfully expressed it, "that he had only to stamp his foot, and soldiers would spring from the soil."

All readers of Roman history are acquainted with the dramatic scene, which displays Cæsar pausing on the banks of the brook Rubicon, until a sudden impulse causes him to plunge into the water, crying, "The die is cast." It is pretty but unfounded, like many other attractive portions of history. Leaving Ravenna at night, he reached **49** Ariminum (*Rimini*) at dawn, and was met there **B.C.** by his devoted friend in the Tribunate, Antony, who had fled from Rome on the night after the passing of the decree.

In a month Cæsar was master of Umbria and Picenum. Then strengthened by two legions from Gaul, he laid siege to Corfinium in the Apennines, where Domitius Brassbeard upheld Pompey's cause. Upon the surrender of the place he treated its defenders with great mildness, and forbade all plunder; a policy which changed many of his opponents into friends.

Meanwhile Pompey had gone to Brundusium, for the purpose of crossing to Greece. Before Cæsar's appearance under the strong fortifications of this place the Consuls had sailed for Dyrrhachium in Epirus; and the baffled general, unable to prevent the embarkation, soon saw the last of Pompey's ships sink below the horizon. Cæsar was thus left master of Italy; but the lack of ships hindered him from pursuing his foe in the meantime.

He turned instead to Spain, where Afranius and Varro maintained the cause of Pompey. Before the autumn he had reduced both sections of the Peninsula. As he passed along the shore of Gaul on his homeward way, he completed the reduction of Marseilles, before which one of his officers had been lying for some time.

When he reached Rome, to act as Dictator for eleven days, and then to receive the Consulship, he heard somewhat discouraging news from other quarters. His lieutenants had been beaten in Illyria; and in Africa Curio, drawn by a *ruse* from the old camp of Scipio, had been defeated and slain. These events left Africa and the East in the hands of the Pompeians, Cæsar holding Italy, Gaul, and Spain.

Fixing his head-quarters at Thessalonica, Pompey had meanwhile been preparing for a great struggle. His hopes were high. Seven legions—abundance of money, food, and stores—and a great fleet to sweep the Adriatic seemed to augur well for success.

On the 5th of November Cæsar crossed from Brundusium to the shore of Epirus with a part of his army. Pompey hurried to save Dyrrhachium; and the two camps were pitched on opposite banks of the Apsus, where they remained during the winter.

The fleet of Pompey under Bibulus kept the sea so well, that Antony could not carry over the rest of Cæsar's force.

BATTLE OF PHARSALIA.

So anxious was the Consul about its arrival, that in the dress of a slave he braved the wintry sea in a small rowing-boat, and fought all night in vain to make the passage. When the oarsmen grew pale at the tumult of the waves, and refused to pull, he encouraged them with the words, "You carry Cæsar and his fortunes." At last he gave up the attempt to cross. When Antony sailed, a contrary wind bore him past Pompey's camp in full view of the enemy, who however could not prevent him, although they pursued, from landing near the headland of Nymphæum, more than fifty miles north of the Apsus. Cæsar made a speedy march to avert the danger resulting from the position of Pompey's camp between Antony and himself. And Pompey, thus outwitted, shifted his camp to a new position, north of Dyrrhachium, and fortified it with a curving line of intrenchments, which faced the land side in a convex form. Cæsar inclosed this position with lines of still greater length, but they were so weak and ill-manned that Pompey easily broke through.

Upon the plain of Pharsalia in Thessaly the decisive action took place. The numbers were unequal, for Pompey had forty-four thousand, while Cæsar's army was scarcely half that number; but Cæsar's men were hardy veterans, while Pompey's force consisted largely of raw recruits. The arm on which Pompey placed most hope was his splendid muster of cavalry. Cæsar's soldiers advanced at a run; but, when they saw the enemy standing still, for Pompey had given orders to wait until the javelins crossed, **48** they halted to take breath. And then both sides B.C. closed in a deadly struggle. To make up for the want of horse, Cæsar had picked out some steady veterans to fight between the cohorts; and to them he is said to have given the singular order to strike at the *faces* of the foe. For, says Plutarch, "these young cavaliers, quite unused to war or wounds, and prizing their beauty highly, would avoid above all things a wound in that part." The order gained its end. The Cavalry, dismayed by the efforts to spoil their beauty, turned and fled. The famous Tenth, hitherto kept in reserve, now came up to break the infantry of Pompey, who retired stupid with despair to his tent. But he was not safe even there; for in a short time the soldiers of Cæsar burst through the defences of his camp, and he left it by one gate, while they were pouring through the other. Cæsar pardoned several of Pompey's followers, who submitted after the battle; and among them, Junius Brutus. Neither he nor the victor who forgave him foresaw a bloody Ides of March, that waited in the future, big with fate for both.

At the mouth of the Peneus Pompey went on board a ship, in which he sailed to Lesbos for his wife Cornelia and his younger son Sextus. Thence he went to Cilicia and afterwards to Cyprus, where he decided on seeking refuge in Egypt, for the Senate had made him guardian of Ptolemy Dionysus and the Princess Cleopatra, children of Ptolemy Auletes. Alexandria was then in the hands of a revolutionary Triumvirate, who had expelled Cleopatra and were governing the country in the name of Ptolemy. The three resolved to kill Pompey; and one of them, Achillas, an Egyptian, went out in a little fishing-boat to the ship, accompanied by two officers, who had once served under Pompey. Desiring him to come into the boat, because the water was too shallow for a galley to row in to the shore, they pushed off, while his wife and son hung over the side of the ship, gazing wistfully at the receding boat. By this time several men in the dress of high officials had come to the beach. Pompey, alarmed at the ominous silence which prevailed in the boat, addressed one of the officers, saying, "I think we once served together in war." A slight nod being the only response, he busied himself with his tablets, on which he had written notes of a speech in Greek, that he intended to make to Ptolemy. When the boat struck the shore, he rose, and at once was run through the body from behind. The shriek of Cornelia rang in his dying ears. When life was extinct, the head was cut off, and the naked body tossed on the sands. His faithful attendant, Philip, having washed off the blood with salt water and wrapped the trunk in his cloak, gathered wood from the wreck of a fishing-boat to make a funeral pile. An old soldier of Pompey came up to share in the mournful toil.

Cæsar, passing across the Hellespont into Asia Minor, reached Egypt soon after Pompey's death. The head and signet-ring of the dead man were carried on board his ship. His eyes filled with tears at the ghastly sight, as he commanded the head to be burned. After he had entered Alexandria, Cleopatra caused herself to be rolled in a bale of carpets and carried secretly into his palace. Her charms soon made the conqueror a willing captive; but the mob of Alexandria, incited by Achillas, who dreaded a reconciliation between the brother and the sister, assailing the palace, drove Cæsar to take refuge in Pharos, where he was blockaded. In one of the conflicts that ensued Cæsar saved his life and his fame as a man of letters by leaping from a sinking skiff, and swimming to one of his galleys with a coat of mail in his teeth, and his manuscripts held high over water in one hand.

The arrival of reinforcements enabled Cæsar to put an end to this Egyptian War. Ptolemy, after a defeat, was drowned in the Nile, upon which Cleopatra was made Queen of Egypt.

Before Cæsar, who delayed long in the seductive society of Cleopatra, left the East, he humbled the pride of Pharnaces, son of Mithridates, in the battle of Zela in Syria (47 B.C.). It was upon this occasion that he sent home the well-known laconic despatch, *Veni: vidi: vici.*

As Dictator, Cæsar found much to do at Rome; but the mutiny of the legions at Capua was the most perilous event of the year. His cool courage and keen insight into character aided him in this crisis. To the lowering ranks that looked upon themselves as necessary to his power—and tried on that ground to extort a gift of money, he cried suddenly, "I discharge you." And in the silence that followed he told them they should have the money, when he came to lead his other troops in triumph. Still severer was the sting of the word *Quirites*, with which, as if they were now civilians, he next began, after dismissing them from his service. After declaring that he must disband the Tenth Legion at least, and thus playing with their fears and their repentance, he tardily consented to overlook their faults and receive their expressions of sorrow.

The Pompeian leaders—Cnæus the eldest son, Cato, Cicero, Scipio, and others—having assembled at Corcyra, resolved to make a stand in Africa. Thither accordingly went Scipio and Cato with a fleet and army. Cato became governor of Utica. Cæsar crossed the sea in the autumn of 47; but it was the following February before the decisive conflict took place at Thapsus, shattering the Pompeian party to pieces. The leaders killed themselves. Juba, King of Numidia, and Petreius, both keen partisans of Pompey, fought a duel after a carouse, for the purpose of finding the death they coveted. The Roman fell, and the African bared his breast to the blade of a slave. But the suicide of Cato was most notable of all. When he heard at Utica of the rout at Thapsus, he resolved to die. Some friendly hand removed his sword from its wonted place at the head of his bed. Sternly commanding it to be brought, he began to read a dialogue of Plato—the *Phædo*—but fell asleep over the scroll. When he awoke, he stabbed himself, but not with a mortal wound. His friends ran in, when they heard him groaning, and a surgeon dressed the wound. But, when left alone, he took off the bandage and tore open the gash, until his bowels gushed out, and then in a short time he died.

Leaving as ruler of Numidia Sallust the historian, Cæsar returned to Rome to enjoy a four-fold Triumph over Gaul, Egypt, Pontus, and Numidia. The arena grew red with the blood of gladiators and wild beasts contending in mortal strife; and on the benches of the amphitheatre clustered men wild with all the joy, which the bestowal of a splendid gift or the removal of a gnawing fear can produce. For amid the showering gifts that rewarded his soldiers and partisans, he gratified his foes with a general pardon.

Created Dictator for ten years—this being the third time he had received the great office—and Censor for three, Cæsar devoted some time to the internal business of the State. From this task he was called away to crush the embers of the Pompeian party in Spain, where were assembled Pompey's two sons along with Labienus and Varro. Driving them from their position at Cordova, he brought them to bay at Munda, a town not far west of Malaga. The conflict was desperate, for the Pompeians knew that it was their last chance. At length

Cæsar won the battle, but not till thirty thousand of his foes cumbered the field. Labienus and Varro were slain. Cnæus Pompey, whose foot was cut instead of the hawser, as he was trying to escape in a boat, was caught among the hills, and put to death. His younger brother Sextus got safely away to the north of the Peninsula. Cæsar then came home to celebrate his fifth Triumph.

His last winter was devoted to statesmanship. Then and during the summer of 46 he passed a number of salutary laws. He relieved the Treasury by revising the register of those who received monthly supplies of grain, and striking many names off the list. He extended the franchise to many districts of Gaul and Spain. He increased the number of the Senate to nine hundred, partly by placing on its benches some of his old soldiers and some citizens of Cisalpine Gaul, who then, as some one sneeringly remarked, "exchanged the trews for the toga." Among his reforms was a change in the Calendar, which brought the confused Roman year of three hundred and fifty-five days, kept straight by inserting months occasionally, up to three hundred and sixty-five days, with the addition of another day every four years.* He also meditated great plans of drainage, engineering, and a Cæsarian Code, all of which were rudely checked by the assassin's dagger.

A growing—and perhaps not unfounded—fear that he aimed at being King, took possession of the popular mind. In various ways he tried to sound the citizens, who saw his head stamped on every coin of the Republic that passed through their hands. Crowns were found one morning on his statues in the Forum, but the people shouted gladly when two of the Tribunes pulled off the emblems of monarchy. A dramatic scene was acted at the Lupercalia or Festival of Pan, when Antony twice offered him a diadem wreathed with laurel, as he sat enthroned in a golden chair. The scanty cheering, when the offer was made, was completely drowned in the thunders of applause that greeted Cæsar's rejection of the toy.

---

* The slight error in the Julian Calendar (which made the year eleven minutes longer than the solar year) was reduced nearly altogether by Pope Gregory in 1582 A.D. We adopted the Gregorian style in 1752.

Cleopatra's visit to Rome with her son Cæsarion—the proposal of a senatorial decree permitting Julius to be styled King in the provinces—and the general discontent of those who were, or conceived themselves to be, injured by his reforms—concurred in leading to the formation of a plot against the life of the Dictator. Marcus Junius Brutus was elected as the fittest leader; and scraps of mysterious writing, urging him to action or taunting him with degeneracy, were frequently found in his Prætorian chair, or affixed to the statue of his great ancestor, who had expelled the Tarquins. Cassius, Casca, Cimber, Decimus Brutus, Trebonius, Ligarius were the other chief conspirators.

The Ides (that is, the 15th) of March* was the appointed day—the Senate-house the scene chosen for the enactment of the tragedy. Many hints and warnings preceded the event, but they were all in vain. A soothsayer told Cæsar to beware of the Ides of March. His wife had dreams so ominous the night before, that she begged him not to go to the Senate-house that morning. But Decimus Brutus, coming in, laughed off his scruples, and induced him to go to the Senate, by assuring him that the title of King everywhere out of Italy was to be conferred on him that day. On his way to the House a slave tried in vain to struggle through the crowd for the purpose of warning him. Artemidorus, a teacher of Greek, handed him a scroll detailing the plot, but he was prevented from reading it by the numerous petitioners who hung upon his steps. Certain words dropped in the crowd alarmed the conspirators, whose fears grew intense, when they saw a Senator, who seemed to know of the plot, whispering in Cæsar's ear. Cassius would have stabbed himself at this moment, had not Brutus bid him watch the gestures of the talker, who was evidently imploring Cæsar to grant a request.

44
B.C.

Then came the opportunity. Cimber knelt down to offer a petition in favour of his banished brother, while the rest of the conspirators crowded round. Cæsar rose somewhat angrily to rebuke them for their forwardness, when Cimber, holding

---

* The Romans called the 1st of every month the *Kalends*. The *Nones* fell on the 5th of all months except March, May, July, and October, when they were on the 7th. The *Ides* were the 15th of these four months,—the 13th of all the rest.

the skirt of his gown, plucked it from his neck, upon which Casca's sword descended. Turning like a wounded tiger, the Dictator saw a score of blades gleaming in his face. Swiftly they stabbed and smote, while he, with a soldier's instinct, held out his left arm all swathed in his gown, and struck fiercely at his assailants with the sharp point of his iron pen. But the sight of Brutus paralyzed his arm. When the dagger of that befriended and trusted man pierced his body, he rolled his mantle round his face, and sank at the foot of Pompey's statue—dying with three-and-twenty wounds. So wildly did the murderers chop and hew at their victim, that some of themselves were wounded by the random strokes.

GREAT NAMES OF THE FIRST CENTURY B.C.

VARRO, "most learned of the Romans"—born 116 B.C.—served under Pompey till after Pharsalia—forgiven then by Cæsar—great friend of Cicero—proscribed by Second Triumvirate, but escaped—died in 28 B.C.—among his very numerous writings may be named *De Re Rustica,* an agricultural treatise, and his *Antiquities, Human and Divine,* the latter being his chief work.

CICERO, M. Tullius (hence sometimes called Tully), greatest of Roman Orators—born at Arpinum 106 B.C.—for his history see pp. 93 to 113—his literary fame rests on his *Speeches* and *Philosophical Works*—his *Poems* were inferior.

CÆSAR, historian—born B.C. 100—for his history see pp. 93 to 107—chief work, the *Commentaries,* relating the story of the Gallic War for seven years, and a part of the Civil War—author also of *Orations, Epistles,* a *Jest-book,* some *Poems,* &c.

LUCRETIUS—didactic poet—born 95 B.C.—author of *De Rerum Natura* in six books, expounding the doctrines of Epicurus—committed suicide about 51 B.C.

CATULLUS, lyric and epigrammatic poet—born at Verona in 87 B.C.—a man of fashion at Rome in the time of Julius Cæsar—died some time later than 47 B.C.—among the finest of his poems may be named the *Nuptials of Peleus and Thetis* and the *Atys,* the latter being considered his masterpiece.

SALLUST, historian—born at Amiternum in B.C. 86—of plebeian extraction—served as Tribune of the Plebs—expelled from the Senate by the Censors in 50 B.C.—governor of Numidia under Cæsar—died 34 B.C.—author of the *Catiline War,* the *Jugurthine War,* and other works.

VITRUVIUS, architectural writer—birth-place uncertain—served under Julius Cæsar in Africa as a military engineer—superintended public buildings under Augustus—author of *De Architectura* in ten books.

VIRGIL, celebrated Latin poet—born at Andes near Mantua in Cisalpine Gaul, B.C. 70—expelled from his farm by one of the soldiers, to whom Octavianus after Philippi assigned land—but afterwards restored—became acquainted with Mæcenas, to whom he introduced Horace—died at Brundusium B.C. 19—great works, the *Æneid,* an epic in twelve books; the *Georgics,* an agricultural poem; the *Eclogues* or *Bucolics,* his earliest work.

HORACE, celebrated Latin poet—born at Venusia in Apulia 65 B.C.—his father a collector of taxes or auction-fees. Educated at Rome and Athens—served as a Tribune under Brutus—his estate confiscated after Philippi—served as a clerk in the Quæstor's office—

received a Sabine farm from Mæcenas—died B.C. 8—his works consist mainly of *Odes, Satires, Epistles,* &c.

LIVY, historian—born at Patavium 59 B.C.—flourished at the court of Augustus—died 17 A.D.—author of *Annales,* a history of Rome from the beginning to the death of Drusus B.C. 9—in 142 books —only 35 have descended to us, but we possess *Epitomes* from an unknown pen of all the rest but two.

TIBULLUS, elegiac poet—born probably 54 B.C.—patronized by Messala, whose aide-de-camp he was in Gaul—friend of Horace—died probably B.C. 18—of the *Elegies* only the first two books are undoubtedly from his pen.

PROPERTIUS, elegiac poet—born in Umbria probably in 51 B.C.— lived a fashionable life at Rome, attached to the circle of Mæcenas —time of death unknown.

OVID, celebrated Latin poet—born at Sulmo, 43 B.C.—held some magistracies, and lived pleasantly at Rome until an edict of Augustus banished him to Tomi on the Euxine, 8 A.D.—the assigned reason, to hide some weightier motive, was his publication of the *Ars Amatoria*—he died there in 18 A.D.—author of the *Metamorphoses* and the *Fasti,* besides *Epistles, Elegies,* &c.

NEPOS, biographer—probably born at Verona—died in the reign of Augustus—supposed author of *Lives of Illustrious Men;* but some think the extant work of biographies is an abbreviation by Probus of a larger work.

PHÆDRUS, a slave of Thrace or Macedonia—lived at Rome under Augustus, who set him free, and Tiberius—author of *Fables* in Latin iambics; the best of these are founded on those ascribed to Æsop.

CHAPTER III.
MARK ANTONY.

The Funeral Speech.	Cleopatra's Galley.
Battle of Mutina.	Defeat of Sextus Pompey.
Second Triumvirate.	Sloth of Antony.
Death of Cicero.	Battle of Actium.
Battle of Philippi.	Death of Antony and Cleopatra.

WHEN Cæsar was dead, the conspirators went through the empty streets of Rome, holding up their bloody swords and crying out, "Liberty." Finding that the populace did not join them, they then retired to the Capitol, to await the movements of Antony and Lepidus, whom they feared. Antony made himself master of Cæsar's money and his parchments.

The hopes of the conspirators rose, when Cicero came to the Capitol to praise their deed, and Cinna the Prætor followed. Coming to the Forum the next day, Brutus made a speech; but, when Cinna following began to blacken Cæsar's name, the angry cries of the crowd made them retire again to the Capitol. A meeting of the Senate then took place, at which Antony moved and Cicero seconded a general amnesty. The passing of this measure lightened the hearts of the chief conspirators, who accepted dinner invitations from Antony and Lepidus—Cassius being the guest of Antony, Brutus of Lepidus.

But the reading of Cæsar's will, in which he named Octavius his heir and bequeathed to every Roman citizen a sum equal to more than £2 of our money, giving besides his gardens beyond Tiber to be a public park, turned the mob fiercely against the assassins.

The smouldering fire of their anger broke into furious flame, when Mark Antony as Consul pronounced his famous funeral speech over the ivory-bier, on which the mangled body was carried to the Forum. When he had sufficiently wrought up the feelings of the crowd by dwelling on the soldiership, the generosity, and the mournful fate of the dead man, he showed them a waxen figure painted to represent the ghastly wounds, and spread before their horror-stricken eyes the very toga Cæsar had worn, all torn and bloody with the rending of the daggers. Before matters reached this crisis, the conspirators had fled; the furious crowd, after burning the body in the Forum on a pile made of broken benches and tables, rushed with torches to the houses of the murderers.

Cæsar's heir now appeared upon the scene. While studying at Apollonia, this youth of nineteen, who was the son of Cæsar's niece Atia, heard of his grand-uncle's murder. He met Antony with a demand for the money, but could get no satisfaction. Raising money nevertheless, he contrived to pay the legacies of the will, a step which pleased the people greatly. Antony quickly perceived in the beardless stripling a formidable foe; and the feeling between them soon led to open rupture. Brutus and Cassius meanwhile, after lingering in Italy all the summer, had gone to Greece.

Cicero then began to hurl against Antony those tremendous speeches called Philippics, which uttered their thunders in the Senate at intervals the whole winter through. His tampering with Cæsar's parchments—all his forgeries and interpolations were laid bare. Antony returned to Cisalpine Gaul, where he laid siege to Mutina; and Octavius collected the veterans of Cæsar in preparation for the approaching struggle.

When Antony heard that the Consuls of 43 B.C. were marching northward in conjunction with Octavius, he made a movement from his trenches and defeated Pansa, who received a mortal wound; but the other Consul Hirtius inflicted a signal defeat upon him some days later; and nothing prevented the destruction of his army but the death of Hirtius in the pursuit.

After this defeat at Mutina Antony crossed the Alps into Narbonese Gaul. The sufferings of the march were great—roots, wild berries, even bark being eaten by the famished troops. But these sufferings were atoned for, when the junction of the army of Lepidus with his own placed Antony at the head of seventeen legions and ten thousand horse.

Octavius, nettled by Cicero's sneer at him as a boy who must be removed, opened secret negotiations with Pompey; and made a bold and successful stroke by appearing in the Campus with his soldiers. The people cheered; the leaders of the Senate fled; and the young man not yet twenty received the honours of the Consulship. By a law then passed he assumed the full name to which he was entitled as Cæsar's heir—Julius Cæsar Octavianus.

Before long Antony, Octavian, and Lepidus met on a little island in the river near Bononia (*Bologna*); and formed there the Second Triumvirate. The partition of the Empire occupied them first—the Gauls, except Narbonese, being allotted to Antony—Spain and Narbonese Gaul to Lepidus—Africa, Sicily, and Sardinia to Octavian. The Consuls of the year (of whom Lepidus was to be one) were to hold Italy. And, as to the East, Antony and Octavian were to proceed at once to wrest it from Brutus and Cassius, who had gone thither and were in arms.

43
B.C.

A List of Blood—a second and worse Proscription—was then drawn up, all ties of relationship and former intimacy giving way before the lust of power. Cicero—Antony's uncle Cæsar—and Paullus the brother of Lepidus—were jotted down to die, amid more than two thousand others. The Triumvirs then went to Rome to slay.

Fleeing from his villa at Tusculum in company with his brother, Cicero got to sea with the purpose of joining Brutus in Macedon. His brother, who ventured back to Rome for money, was slain. The aged orator could not help landing to spend a night in his villa at Formiæ, whence his slaves could scarcely induce him to move next day. As they were bearing him in a litter through the shadowy woodlands to the shore, a noise was heard behind; and Antony's soldiers, who had already ransacked the villa and were put on the scent by one whom Cicero had educated, came running after them. The old man bade the bearers set the litter down; and, as the pursuers came on, they beheld his tangled grey hair and wasted cheek peering through the curtains, as, leaning his chin upon his hand, he gazed at them with a steadfast eye. Stretching out his neck when they came up, he received a fatal blow from the centurion's sword. Thus died the greatest of Latin orators at the age of sixty-four. By Antony's express desire his head, and the hands which had written the Philippics, were cut off. These noble parts of the dead body were brought to Rome, and nailed to the Rostra. We learn how even the women of the time were brutalized, when we read that Fulvia, formerly the wife of Clodius and now the wife of Antony, drew out her golden hair-pin, when she saw the gory head, and stuck it through the tongue, once so eloquent.

Brutus had meanwhile gone to his province of Macedonia, and Cassius to that of Syria, where they maintained themselves in spite of Antony's efforts to expel them in favour of his own partisans. They became masters of the East; but wasted much time in levying contributions forcibly among the cities of Asia Minor. Meeting upon a certain occasion at Sardis, they had a bitter quarrel, which Shakspere has immortalized in that drama, which he should have called *Brutus* after its real hero. While Brutus was on his way back to Europe, he saw an apparition in the dead of night, which, as he looked up quietly from his book and asked, "Whence art thou?" told him with a frown, "I am thy evil genius. We shall meet at Philippi." The spectre must have been the creation of a mind, stained with blood, acting on a body, worn out with care and want of sleep.

When the Triumviral army approached Philippi, Brutus and Cassius had mustered a force of one hundred thousand men; but they lacked good officers. Among the students at Athens they had recruited largely, one of their raw tribunes being the young Horace afterwards so distinguished as a poet. The Republicans occupied two hills by the sea; the Triumviral army, which soon began to feel the pinch of famine, was posted in the swampy plain.

Antony having commenced works to cut Cassius off from the sea, Brutus urged the need of an attack and gained his point against the will of Cassius. Brutus, leading his men successfully against the army of Octavian, who lay sick, even broke into the camp; but Cassius was driven back with loss by Antony. Anxious to know the fortune of his colleague, Brutus sent a body of cavalry to ask Cassius how he had fared; but the dispirited leader, mistaking them for foes, went into his tent, and, according to the common account, got his freedman Pindarus to kill him. Lost in sad thoughts Brutus stood over his dead associate, and, turning away with a sigh, said, "There lies the last of the Romans."

42 B.C.

Twenty days later, Brutus, who had no talent as a general, led his army out against the Triumvirs, although by declining a battle he might easily have exhausted their strength by famine. He was beaten by the superior numbers they had collected. The next day his men refused to fight, upon which he went into a wood accompanied by some friends, whom he vainly besought to slay him. At last with much difficulty he induced a Greek freedman to hold a sword, on which he flung himself. His wife Portia, daughter of Cato, afterwards killed herself by putting live charcoal into her mouth.

The character of Brutus as depicted by Shakspere is not historical. We must lay aside the pure patriotism and noble self-devotion of that great creation, before we arrive at a true estimate of the man, who plunged into Cæsar's body the worst of all the blades that shed his life. He was very fond of books and was free from the deep profligacy of the age; this is nearly all the praise that history awards him.

The victors of Philippi divided the Empire between them —Antony taking the East, Octavian the West as his share. To Lepidus was left merely Africa.

Antony, making a progress through Asia Minor, arrived at Tarsus. There he learned that Cleopatra, whom he had summoned to appear before him on the charge of having aided Cassius in the war, was approaching. She came resolved to conquer. A barge, all shining with gold, propelled by sails of purple silk and oars of silver, bore her to the music of flutes and harps up the Cydnus. Dressed as Venus and fanned by Cupids, she reclined with languishing grace under an awning bright with gold, while beautiful girls, in the guise of Nereids and Graces, hovered round, playing at the management of the galley, from whose deck blue clouds of burning perfume rose with sweet dimness through the air. This artful princess soon induced Antony to accompany her to Alexandria, where he lived for a while in a whirl of luxurious pleasure.

From this trance he was roused by news that his fiery wife Fulvia and his brother Lucius, obliged by Agrippa the lieutenant of Octavian to surrender Perusia, whither they had fled, had left Italy, after a vain effort to withstand the power of the young Triumvir. Further startled by tidings from the East, where Labienus, fighting under the Parthian banner, was overrunning Syria and Asia Minor victoriously, he shook off the silken chains of Cleopatra for a time, and after visiting Tyre went to Athens, where were met his wife, his brother, and many Romans discontented with Octavian. A new Civil War might have broken out, had not the death of Fulvia removed an obstacle to peace. Antony and Octavian met once more as friends, the union being cemented by a marriage between Antony and Octavia, the sister of his colleague. By this peace, named from Brundusium, the boundary between East and West was fixed at Scodra in Illyricum.

Sextus Pompey, younger son of the Triumvir, had ere this established himself in Sicily, whence he made piratical excursions. Before the peace of Brundusium Antony had sought his aid; but that compact decided that Octavian should expel him from Sicily, while Antony was warring in Parthia. Pompey in his anger cut off the supplies of corn which the Romans usually drew from Sicily ; and bread-riots became frequent in the capital. The Triumvirs were thus forced to make terms with Sextus, on one of whose ships they assembled at Misenum. The result of the conference left him ruler of Sicily, Sardinia, Corsica, and Achaia.

But the last portion of territory was soon refused by Antony; and a naval war with Sextus began (38 B.C.). He had the best of the struggle, until Octavian committed its conduct to Agrippa, a man of talent and energy. This officer spent two years in making the Julian Port by connecting the Lakes Lucrinus and Avernus with the sea, and in collecting a sufficient fleet. Three squadrons in the summer of 36 B.C. prepared to descend on the three shores of Sicily. That of Lepidus only effected a landing, storms having driven back Octavian and Agrippa. At Mylæ Sextus and Agrippa met; but the former, drawing off most of his ships, darted upon Octavian and scattered his squadron. Agrippa followed; and inflicted so signal a defeat upon Sextus near the Straits of Messana, that the beaten sailor was forced to flee to Lesbos. Crossing to Asia afterwards, he was taken and slain by the officers of Antony.

The Parthian War had been meanwhile proceeding successfully under Ventidius, an officer of merit who had originally been a dealer in mules. In two campaigns this general won several battles and slew both Labienus, the Roman renegade, and Pacorus, son of the Parthian King. When Antony came from Athens to supersede his lieutenant, the siege of Samosata was in progress. The Triumvir took the command, but met so fierce a resistance that he was glad to take from the besieged prince a sum much smaller than had been offered to his lieutenant. He then returned to Athens; while Ventidius went to Rome to enjoy a Triumph.

After the defeat of Sextus Pompey Lepidus made a feeble movement towards independence; but Octavian's swift descent upon his camp deprived him of his troops, and reduced him to that obscurity, out of which he should never have come.

Antony now flung the reins of self-control completely aside, and suffered his passion for Cleopatra to drag him swiftly to destruction. Inviting her to Syria, he bestowed on her several provinces, embracing nearly all the eastern coasts of the Levant. Before he sank quite into ignoble indolence, he made an effort to curb the Parthians. Marching into the heart of Asia, he gained some trifling successes; but, owing to bad plans, severe sicknesses, and the error of leaving part of his troops behind, only to be destroyed, he became so entangled in perils, that he was forced to make a costly retreat into Armenia. He cared little so that he got back to Cleopatra. Next year he invaded Armenia, lately in alliance with him, and carried back the King to decorate an Alexandrian Triumph.

For three years Antony loitered at the court of Cleopatra, idling and feasting his time away. How silly he had grown may be judged from a story related by Plutarch. While fishing one day along with the Queen, he waited so long for a bite and was so vexed at his want of success in her presence, that he sent a diver down to put on his hook a fish that he had caught before. She saw through the trick, but pretended to wonder at his invariable success. As there was another fishing-party next day, she collected a number of her friends, avowedly to see Antony's marvellous success, but in reality to have a good laugh at him. He let down his line, and waited. There came a tug. Pulling quickly up, he found on the hook—a salted fish, which she had ordered a diver of *her* choosing to place there. So much for the folly of these days. Their reckless luxury may be judged from her celebrated draught of vinegar, in which a priceless pearl had been dissolved. But he did things more irritating to the Romans at home than these absurdities. He stamped Cleopatra's head with his own upon the coins he issued. He placed a Herod on the throne of Judæa by his own sole authority. He made Polemo, the illegitimate offspring of his amour with Cleopatra, King of Armenia.

Octavian, meanwhile, in the West had been gaining strength and reputation. By his victories over the Dalmatians and Pannonians he cleared the province of Illyricum, and extended the Roman rule in that direction to the Save.

The two men, who divided the Roman world, had gradually become estranged. Antony's treatment of Octavia was a source of much anger on the part of her brother Octavian, who lost no opportunity of dwelling in the Senate on his colleague's assumption of Oriental splendour and compliance with every whim of his Egyptian mistress, who really ruled the East through her indolent paramour. Recrimination widened the breach. Antony accused Octavian of having seized Sicily and Africa without giving him a share. Octavian replied that Antony had possessed himself of Egypt and Armenia, and was wasting the resources of Rome in the East upon a worthless woman. It is little wonder that war grew out of these things.

In 32 B.C. the Roman Senate authorized Octavian to make

war upon Cleopatra, through whom they meant to strike at Antony. Stirred at last to action, the voluptuary sent Canidius with his legions into Epirus, and collected a fleet with which, accompanied by Cleopatra, he sailed to Corcyra. Agrippa, commanding Octavian's fleet, cruised about the Ionian Sea, upon which Antony brought his ships to anchor in the Ambracian Gulf, on the northern arm of which his soldiers were encamped. After some consultation, in which, as usual, Cleopatra's will prevailed, it was resolved to trust to the fleet alone as a means of escape. High winds prevented any movement for four days. But on the fifth (Sept. 2) Antony's vessels, which were huge and heavy, like those of the Armada in later history, began to move out; and Octavian's light ships, unable to bear the shock of an encounter beak to beak with such enormous hulls, clustered round the great wooden castles and plied them with missiles, as in a land fight. At this crisis Cleopatra's squadron of sixty ships broke the line, with all sails set, and made for the south. Antony, long used to follow whither this dark enchantress led, fled after her in a swift quinquereme. The battle was over; the remainder of the fleet was destroyed; the army surrendered.

31
B.C.

When Antony went on board the galley, in which the Egyptian Queen had fled, he refused at first to see her; but in a few days fell into his old habits of intimacy. Together they fled to Africa, whither Octavian followed at his leisure. In this crisis of fortune Cleopatra showed some spirit; Antony had none. She had wild dreams of carrying her ships across the sandy plain of Suez, and seeking some distant shore. Upon the abandonment of this scheme she tried to cajole Octavian, as she had cajoled Cæsar and Antony; but all her wiles fell blunt and harmless. Antony shut himself up in a small lodge in Pharos on the very margin of the sea.

When Octavian entered Alexandria (Aug. 1, 30 B.C.) he received imploring messages from both his conquered foes. Antony, who had no hope, heard a false rumour that Cleopatra, having shut herself in a tomb, was dead. Plunging a dagger into his breast, he asked to be laid beside her. He was drawn up with ropes; and she lavished tears and tenderness on him until he died. She then tried her arts and blandishments once more upon Octavian; but she saw neither pity nor passion in the cold gaze he turned upon her. She knew that he meant to drag her in chains through the streets of Rome in order to gratify the people with a sight of that faded beauty, whose charms had so besotted and enslaved their greatest men. When the soldiers of Octavian, alarmed by a letter she wrote, broke open her bolted door, they found her in queenly dress lying dead upon a golden couch, while one of her women, with dying hand, was arranging the crown upon her brow. The common story is that a peasant brought her an asp, hidden in a basket of figs, and that she let it bite her breast or arm. She was in her thirty-ninth year.

CHAPTER IV.

THE REIGN OF AUGUSTUS.

Called Augustus.	Wars of Augustus.
His Ministers.	The Legions of Varus.
Works of Peace.	Domestic Life.
The Prætorian Guards.	Death of Augustus.

A TIME of peace, whether in the history of a nation or in that of an individual, is a time barren in events. Such a period in Roman history we have now reached. The storm of the Civil Wars is over; the calm of the Augustan Age has begun.

Returning from Egypt, Octavian celebrated a Triumph of three days. Some of his advisers counselled him to retire from the cares of public life; but, fortunately for Rome, other counsels prevailed. Gradually under his administration, while the forms of the old Republic remained, all the offices and powers centred in a single individual. Consul, Tribune for life, Censor and Proconsul in all the provinces, Pontifex Maximus, all these influential positions fell one by one into the hands of the conqueror of Antony, who now vanishes from the page of history as Octavian, for the title of Augustus (meaning sacred or venerable) was conferred on him in the year 27 B.C., and by this name he was henceforth called. The military title of *Imperator* was also conferred upon him for ten years. The bestowal of these honourable names is generally regarded as marking the opening of his reign.

Augustus owed much of the quiet splendour of his reign to the ministers, by whom he was surrounded. Of these four were chief—Agrippa, Mæcenas, Messala, and Pollio. Of Agrippa we have heard already. Mæcenas, the friend and patron of Virgil and Horace, was a knight of Etrurian descent. Messala, celebrated by Tibullus, and Pollio, distinguished as orator, poet, and historian, also contributed to the glory of the time.

WORKS OF AUGUSTUS.

The works of Augustus were chiefly works of peace. The city was so much embellished by public buildings that this first of the Emperors was accustomed towards the end of his reign to boast that "he had found Rome built of brick, and left it built of marble." The regulation of the police, the repair of the great roads, the reduction of the Senate to six hundred members, and the absorption of its functions into a kind of Privy-council, which he controlled himself, occupied his time. To him was due the institution of the Prætorian Guards, a body of ten cohorts, each consisting of eight hundred or one thousand men, horse and foot, set apart with double pay and peculiar privileges for the protection of the Emperor's person. Augustus kept only three cohorts in the city, scattering the rest through Italy; but we shall find Tiberius drawing them all to the centre, and establishing them in a permanent camp near Rome.

In spite of the mildness with which Augustus ruled, several plots were formed against his life; so that his peace of mind was clouded, like that of Cromwell in later days, with fears of assassination, owing to which he wore a breastplate under his robe, whenever he went to a meeting of the Senate.

The wars of Augustus were chiefly in the remote European provinces. He spent three years in Spain (27-24 B.C.), engaged in subduing the wild tribes of the Asturias. The city of Saragossa (a corruption of *Cæsar Augusta*) was founded as a monument of the war. The task of conquering Spain was completed by Agrippa in 19 B.C.

Augustus dwelt for a couple of winters at Samos, during one of which (in 20 B.C.) there were great rejoicings at the restoration by the Parthians of the standards and prisoners taken from Crassus and from Antony.

Throughout all the reign a war was raging among the Alps and on the Rhine. Drusus, the stepson of the Emperor, undertook the conquest of Germany in 12 B.C.; and had proceeded victoriously northward through the forests as far as the Elbe, when want of provisions compelled him to retreat. A fall from his horse caused his death in 9 B.C. His brother Tiberius then took the command, and succeeded in reducing the tribes between the Weser and the Rhine.

A war in Pannonia and Dalmatia turned him from the Rhine to the land between the Adriatic and the Danube. During the occurrence of these things there happened at Bethlehem, in Judæa, an event, before which all others in history except one three and thirty years later, sink into utter insignificance. Jesus Christ, "God made manifest in the flesh," was born of the Virgin Mary. The best chronology places this event three years-before the commencement of the Christian Era.

3 B.C.

The greatest military event of the reign of Augustus was the disastrous defeat of Varus in Germany. This avaricious and arrogant governor was induced by Hermann (called Arminius by the Romans), a chieftain of the Cheruscan tribe, who had lived as a youth at Rome, and received a military education there, to march against some tribes which had risen in revolt between the Rhine and the Elbe. The march proceeded through swamps that grew deeper and forests that grew thicker every mile, until in a dark and dense place, probably near the sources of the Ems and the Lippe, a host of Germans, led by Hermann, assailed the Legions on all sides at once, and after having thinned their ranks by missiles for two days, made a final and destructive charge upon the third. Scarcely a Roman lived to tell the dreadful tale; all the eagles were taken; and Varus in despair stabbed himself to death. Well might Augustus wring his hands, when he heard the news, and utter the vain and bitter cry," Give me back my Legions, Varus, give me back my Legions." The kites of the Teutoburg forest and the vermin of the marsh were feeding leagues away upon their mangled limbs.

9 A.D.

There was fear in Rome that the victorious Germans would now descend upon the centre of the empire. But there could be no permanent union among the roving swarms. Tiberius and his nephew Germanicus found it impossible to do more than guard the line of the River Rhine and keep the Germans to their own side of the current. But this sufficed to abate the fears at Rome.

Augustus was not happy in his domestic life. The deaths of Mæcenas, Horace, and Virgil, were severe blows to their imperial friend. Still deeper were the wounds of his nephew

Marcellus' death, and the premature decease of his two grandsons, Caius and Lucius Cæsar, all of whom his third wife Livia was by some suspected of having removed by poison. But he had to bear sorrows worse than those caused by death. His daughter Julia, and her daughter, bearing the same name, became so notorious in Rome for profligacy that he was obliged to banish both at different times to islands off the Italian coast.

Augustus died at Nola, 14 A.D. When he felt that death was near, he asked those who stood around his couch, if he had played his part in life well, adding, "If you think so, give me your applause." At the time of his decease he was seventy-seven years of age.

14 A.D.

GREAT NAMES OF THE FIRST CENTURY, A.D.

PLINY (the Elder), naturalist—born 23 A.D. either at Como or Verona—served in Africa, Germany, and Spain—stationed as Admiral of the fleet at Misenum, when Vesuvius burst into its celebrated eruption in 79 A.D.—going ashore to examine the phenomenon he was suffocated by fumes of sulphur—author of *Historia Naturalis* in thirty-seven books.

COLUMELLA, writer on rural affairs—native of Cadiz—lived early in the first Christian century—author of Treatises on *Agriculture, Trees, &c.*

SILIUS ITALICUS, Roman poet (about 25 A.D.-100 A.D.)—distinguished as an advocate—Consul in 68, and afterwards Proconsul of Asia—starved himself to death—chief work *Punica*, an heroic poem in seventeen books.

PERSIUS, satirist—born 34 A.D. at Volaterrae in Etruria—died 62 A.D.—author of six extant *Satires*, in all only 650 lines.

MELA (Pomponius), geographer—native of a town on the Bay of Algesiras in Spain—flourished probably under Claudius—author of *De Situ Orbis.*

SENECA, Stoic philosopher—born at Cordova a few years B.C.—banished to Corsica by Claudius—tutor of Nero—involved in Piso's plot—died by opening his veins 65 A.D.—wrote on *Anger, Consolation, Tranquillity of Mind,* &c.—author also of *Epistles to Lucilius*—chief work, *De Beneficiis,* in seven books.

PETRONIUS, a companion and officer of Nero—killed himself by opening his veins, when accused of treason—supposed author of *Petronii Arbitri Satyricon,* a comic romance of great indecency.

LUCAN, poet—born at Cordova 39 A.D.—engaged in the conspiracy of Piso in reign of Nero—killed himself by opening his veins—only extant work, *Pharsalia,* an heroic poem in ten books, beginning with the passage of the Rubicon.

QUINTILIAN, rhetorician—born about 40 A.D. at Calagurris in Northern Spain—great teacher of eloquence at Rome—died 118 A.D.—chief work, *Institutes of Oratory,* a system of Rhetoric in twelve books.

MARTIAL, born at Bilbilis in Spain 43 A.D.—lived thirty-five years at Rome in the time of Titus and Domitian—distinguished for his witty *Epigrams*—died about 104 A.D.

FLACCUS (Valerius), native of Padua—flourished under Vespasian and Titus—author of *Argonautica,* an unfinished heroic poem.

JUVENAL, poetical satirist—little known of his life—flourished towards close of first century—Aquinum, perhaps his birthplace, was his chosen residence—author of sixteen *Satires* in heroic hexameters.

TACITUS, historian—time and place of birth unknown—married Agricola's daughter, A.D. 78—died at Rome later than 117 A.D.—friend of the younger Pliny—chief works, *Life of Agricola*, *Histories*, extending from 68 A.D. to the death of Domitian, and *Annals*, from the death of Augustus to the death of Nero—wrote also on the *Germans* and the *Decline of Eloquence*.

PLINY (the Younger), nephew of Pliny the Elder—born about 61 A.D., probably at Como—friend of Tacitus—consul in 100 A.D.—author of *Epistles* and a *Panegyric on Trajan*.

SUETONIUS, biographer—probably born soon after Nero's death, 68 A.D.—acted as Secretary to Hadrian—chief work, *Lives of the Cæsars*.

CHAPTER V.

THE UNWORTHY CÆSARS.

Germanicus.	Caractacus.
Sejanus.	Cruelties of Nero.
Island of Capreæ.	Boadicea.
Freaks of Caligula.	The Great Fire.
Claudius Invades Britain.	A wretched Coward.

TWELVE Cæsars are commonly spoken of, but only four of the Emperors who followed Augustus belonged to the line of Julius. These were Tiberius, Caligula, Claudius, and Nero—all in different ways unworthy of the great name.

TIBERIUS, the stepson of Augustus, owed his quiet accession to the imperial throne to the schemes of his mother Livia, who incurred the suspicion of having poisoned many to clear the way for her favourite. Germanicus, his nephew and adopted son, then in command of the legions in Germany, was urged by his soldiers to assume the imperial purple. Instead of doing so he devoted himself more earnestly to the German War, in the hope of removing from the Roman arms the stain caused by the defeat of Varus. He captured the wife of Arminius, penetrated to the forest of Teutoburg, where the Roman dead yet strewed the marshy ground, and in 16 A.D. inflicted a severe defeat on Arminius at Idistavisus near the Weser. These victories pleased the Roman people, but excited the jealousy of dark-souled Tiberius, who recalled him from his command in Germany and sent him to the East. A person named Piso was appointed governor of Syria at the same time, in order that he and his wife might undermine the glories of Germanicus, or perhaps cause his death. Germanicus conquered in the East as he had conquered in the West. A journey to Egypt excited the wrath of Tiberius, who complained that his leave had not been obtained. Matters grew to an open quarrel between Germanicus and Piso; and, when in 19 A.D. the former died near Antioch, there were few who doubted that the cause of death was poison administered by Piso and his wife. Piso's sudden death, when the matter began to be investigated, was ascribed to the desire of Tiberius to be rid of the instrument of a secret crime.

Eleven years of this reign (20–31 A.D.) are filled with the atrocities of a Prefect of the Prætorian Guards named Sejanus, who first induced the Emperor to collect all the Prætorians within a fixed barrack at Rome, and then urged his retirement from Rome to some secret place, where he could practise his debaucheries and commit his cruelties while wrapped in mysterious seclusion. The beautiful island of Capreæ, sleeping in the purple sea, was the den chosen by this imperial wild beast; and there he lived, leaving no mark upon the age he belonged to except in the vacant places of those he slew and the maimed limbs of those he tortured. Sejanus meanwhile was master of Rome; and his statues surpassed those of the Emperor in number. Poison, the stiletto, exile, starvation, torture—every weapon of tyranny came readily to the hand of this monster, who spared neither age nor sex among his foes. But one day from the secret island came a letter to the Senate, accusing Sejanus of treason and ordering his death. That night his mangled body was floating in the Tiber; and his statues were lying in fragments by their pedestals (31 A.D.).

26 A.D.

A man quite as bad named Macro stepped into the vacant place; and the Emperor, as his bodily strength failed from indolence and sensuality, grew more tigerish than before. A young man, Caius, son of Germanicus, who had escaped the slaughters of Sejanus, gained admission to the imperial villa; and when Tiberius, sunk in lethargic sleep, seemed upon the point of death, caused himself to be proclaimed Emperor with the assistance of Macro. But Tiberius rallied; upon which the guilty pair, to save their heads and secure the throne, smothered the old tyrant with pillows. All Rome rang with joy (37 A.D.).

REIGN OF CALIGULA.—We have now for four years (37–41 A.D.) to watch the freaks of a madman, who made the name of Emperor contemptible. Caius, son of Germanicus, is always called Caligula in history from the military boots (*caligæ*) he wore when young. We shall not waste words upon a Roman ruler, who raised his horse *Incitatus* to the Consulship and (A.D. 40) led an army to the northern coast of Gaul, and, setting them to gather shells in their helmets, called it a conquest of Britain. But he was worse than silly. He used to carry a box, from which he offered a pinch to a senator or magistrate now and then. Whoever accepted the offer, died, for the powder was poison; whoever refused, was handed over to the headsman. This official was trained to watch every nod and beck of the Emperor; and, when he saw a certain twist of the finger or an emphatic nod towards any person, he seized his victim at once. It was this Emperor who uttered the savage wish that the whole Roman people had only one neck, that he might slay them all at a blow. At the Palatine games of 41 A.D., after he had enjoyed the delight of watching his subjects scramble for fruit which he flung to them, and while he was going through a vaulted gallery of the palace to the bath Chærea, a Prætorian captain stabbed him with a dagger, and other conspirators, closing round, completed the murder.

REIGN OF CLAUDIUS.—Claudius, uncle of Caligula, being placed on the throne by the Prætorians, might have left a fair reputation in history, had he not been married to the depraved Messalina, who, combined with other evil counsellors, made him commit cruel deeds. He was a man of literary tastes, and had some skill ·in architecture and engineering, in spite of the weakness of mind ascribed to him. Messalina at last overtaxed the patience, which her worst immoralities had failed to break, by causing a young Roman knight to be publicly married to her in 48 A.D. Claudius killed her, and married his niece Agrippina, widow of Domitius Brassbeard. This widow had a son Nero, whom she induced Claudius to adopt as his heir and successor. Seneca the philosopher and Burrus a newly appointed Prefect of Prætorians were made tutors and guardians of this young prince.

The most notable military events of the reign of Claudius were connected with Britain, which was now beginning in earnest to attract the Roman eagles. Sending his lieutenant before him, Claudius in person crossed the strait we call that of Dover. Camulodunum was taken; and the Emperor adopted the surname of Britannicus. But the real work of this British War fell to Vespasian and his son Titus, who drove the noble Celtic chief Caractacus into Wales, and subdued nearly all the southern part of the island. For nine years Caractacus bravely maintained the struggle, until a false kinswoman betrayed him to the Romans. As he was led in chains through Rome he broke into a bitter exclamation—"How could men who dwell in palaces like these envy me a humble cottage in Britain?" Claudius was so struck by his undaunted bearing in adversity that he spared his life (51 A.D.). **43 A.D.**

Dreading from some words of Claudius that he intended to alter his mind regarding Nero, Agrippina got the assistance of a poisoner to prepare death for him in a dish of mushrooms. The drug caused only a fit of retching, upon which his physician brought his reign to an end by painting the inside of his throat with a poisoned feather on pretence of curing the attack (54 A.D.).

REIGN OF NERO.—Tiberius was a morose tyrant—Caligula a fantastic tyrant—Claudius a foolish tyrant—Nero (worst of the four) a dainty and artistic tyrant. By concealing the death of Claudius until the Prætorians had been won over with rich gifts, Agrippina secured the throne for her son of seventeen. For five years he ruled with mildness; but this must be ascribed rather to the fact that his nature had not yet ripened than to any early goodness in the man.

When old enough, he turned upon his mother, who wished to rule through her son, and drew from her the angry threat that she would shift her support to his rival Britannicus, son of Claudius. Nero began his dreadful career by causing this boy to be poisoned. His next step was to remove his mother. Enticing her on board a boat, constructed so as to come to pieces in the water, some of his dependents rowed her out into the sea at Baiæ, and drew out the pegs. She managed to swim ashore and get to her villa; but assassins went thither and slew her in her bed.

The exile and murder of his wife Octavia to make room

for the profligate Poppæa, whom he afterwards kicked to death, formed a natural sequel to these crimes.

The campaigns of Paulinus in Britain belong to Nero's reign. Penetrating to Mona (*Anglesea*) he destroyed the Druid superstition there, and returned to the eastern part of the island just in time to check the rebellion kindled by Boadicea, Queen of the Iceni. This Amazon of old British history, seeing the Roman legions victorious among the marshes of Essex, ended her life by poison (61 A.D.).

A great fire, lasting for six days, consumed the greater part of Rome in this reign. The common scandal of the time ascribed the conflagration to Nero, who, it was said, desired to see how Troy looked when burning, and sang verses from Homer to the music of his harp, as he gazed from a tower upon the sweeping floods of flame and smoke. Nero himself charged the fire upon the Christians, against whom accordingly he set on foot a fearful persecution. In a place made vacant by the flames he built a palace called the Golden House, with tiles and wall-plating of gold, inlaid with gems and mother-of-pearl.

64
A.D.

This Emperor excited the contempt of the Roman aristocracy by his desire to shine as a charioteer and a harper. He performed upon the stage at Naples, and at a later period passed over to Greece for the purpose of appearing at the Olympic and Isthmian Games. It was not pleasant to contend with him, as one singer found who suffered death, because his voice was louder than Nero's.

The discovery of a conspiracy, headed by Piso, gave Nero an opportunity of killing his old tutor Seneca, who with the poet Lucan was involved in the plot. These celebrated men were permitted as a favour to kill themselves by cutting their veins and allowing themselves to bleed to death.

A general, named Galba, having assumed the purple in Gaul, 68 A.D., was recognised by the Prætorians in opposition to Nero. The tyrant, sitting at supper when he heard the news, kicked down two crystal vases in his terror. He called for Locusta to poison him. He called in vain for a gladiator to stab him. He made a sudden rush to the Tiber, but stopped in terror on the bank. As he was riding, with a veil upon his face, to the villa of Phaon, lightning flashed around him, and passing travellers filled him with terror. He unsheathed two daggers, but could not summon courage to plunge them into his breast. Nor was it until the trampling hoofs of horsemen, approaching to slay him, forced him to desperation, that the coward could summon courage to hold a dagger to his throat. Even then the mortal thrust was given by a secretary, who pushed his hand with force enough to drive in the point (A.D. 68).

CHAPTER VI.
TO THE FALL OF ROME.

Jerusalem Destroyed.	Purple for Sale.	Julian and Theodosius.
Agricola in Britain.	Aurelian and Zenobia.	Goths, Vandals, Huns.
Trajan.	Diocletian.	Fall of Rome.
The Antonines.	Constantine the Great.	

WITHIN two years after Nero's miserable death, three generals—the aged and penurious Galba—the effeminate Otho—the beastly Vitellius—wore the purple, and stained it with their blood. The imperial power had now fallen into the hands of the soldiers, who in reality decided the succession.

Vespasian, a general who had won glory in British wars, and was in Palestine preparing to besiege Jerusalem, was declared Emperor in 69 A.D.

The great event of his ten years' reign was the siege and destruction of Jerusalem by his son Titus. A Jewish rebellion had broken out in the reign of Nero; and in the year 70 A.D. the Roman eagles gathered round their prey. From April to August in that dreadful year the wretched Jews underwent unutterable miseries, until the flames of the burning Temple reddened the sky, and the plough passed over the blackened heaps of ruin. The Arch of Titus at Rome still commemorates his victory.

70 A.D.

During the reign of Vespasian, Julius Agricola—the only Roman who can be truly called a conqueror in Britain—entered upon the first of his seven campaigns, 78 A.D.

Titus, succeeding his brave and beneficent father in 79 A.D., held the imperial sceptre until 81 A.D. He was scarcely settled on the throne, when Vesuvius broke into terrific eruption, withering Herculaneum and Stabiæ with streams of molten lava, and showering a fatal rain of hot ashes on Pompeii. Excavations at the base of Vesuvius still supply us with our chief specimens of ancient art and industry, dug from the ruins of those buried towns. The elder Pliny, famed as a naturalist, lost his life by venturing among the sulphureous fumes of the volcano.

Titus, dying of a fever, was succeeded by his frivolous and cruel brother Domitian, one of whose chief pastimes was the spearing of flies with a needle. He persecuted the Christians. The only renown of this reign was due to Agricola, who won the great battle of the Grampians over Galgacus, a Caledonian chief; and who also, by means of his fleet, established the fact that Britain is an island. Domitian treated Agricola as Tiberius had treated Germanicus, ordering him home in a fit of jealous rage, and, as some assert, procuring his death after a time. This Emperor, taking the field in person, was defeated by both the Dacians and the Marcomanni. Yet no reverse could humble him, nor did he shrink from adopting the name *Dominus et Deus*, and ordering worship to be offered at his shrine. A conspiracy, set on foot partly by his wife, led to his assassination in 96 A.D.

84 A.D.

The people and soldiers then made quiet old Nerva Emperor; but in two years a fever prepared the way for the accession of one of the very few great soldiers of the later Empire, Trajan the Spaniard, who reigned from 98 to 117 A.D.

Under this distinguished man Rome enjoyed prosperity. He beautified the city with buildings, erected bridges, and cut roads throughout the provinces; nor was he unmindful of intellectual greatness, as he proved by the establishment of the Ulpian Library.

Refusing to pay the tribute wrested from craven Domitian by the Dacian King, Trajan carried the eagles victoriously across the Danube, over which he cast a stone bridge. The King Decebalus, being beaten at all points after four years' campaigning, committed suicide; and Dacia was made a Roman province. Trajan's Column still commemorates the triumph of the Spanish Emperor. About ten years later Trajan conquered Parthia and Armenia. Having fallen ill in Arabia, he was hurrying home; but he died at Selinus in Cilicia 117 A.D.

104 A.D.

A golden urn containing his ashes was placed under the base of his triumphal column.

Hadrian, the next Emperor, was chiefly remarkable for the incessant journeys he made from one limit of the empire to another. During seventeen years he continued to traverse the ancient world from the Tyne to the Nile, from the Tagus to the Euphrates, examining carefully into the condition of the provincial governments. In northern Britain he left an enduring monument of his visit in the great military wall of masonry he built from the Solway to the Tyne.

131 A.D. The publication of *Edictum Perpetuum*, a code of laws prepared by Salvius Julianus, was among the great events of Hadrian's reign.

A Jewish rebellion breaking out in Syria cost many years and lives; nor did it seem safe to the Emperor to allow the nation to cluster again round the ruins of their fallen city. They were accordingly scattered by an edict forbidding them to live near Jerusalem.

When Hadrian died of dropsy in 138 A.D., his adopted son, Antoninus Pius, began a calm and uneventful reign of three-and-twenty years. He was succeeded in 161 A.D. by Aurelius Antoninus the Philosopher. Mutterings of the great storm of barbaric rage, which finally smote down Pagan Rome, could even then be heard upon the frontiers of the Empire. Aurelius, who had raised his adopted brother Verus to a full share of his power, sent him to fight the Parthians in the East. But a fiercer war arose with two German tribes, the Marcomanni and the Quadi. Placing his head-quarters in Pannonia, Aurelius directed all his energies against these formidable foes. The greatest of his victories was that won over the Quadi in 174 A.D. This war was yet unfinished, when death seized Aurelius at Vienna, 180 A.D.

The third and last of the Antonines was the wretched Commodus, son of Aurelius. The debaucheries of Rome proving irresistible to this youth, upon his father's death he bought peace from the wild Germans, and hurried away to the capital. The dress of a gladiator or a charioteer would have suited him better than the purple he disgraced.

In cruelty and licentiousness he rivalled the worst of Eastern despots. Patience at last reached its limit. A dwarf came running one day to Marcia, mistress of Commodus, with a list of death, containing her own and other names. She mixed a cup of poison for the tyrant; but it seemed to work so slowly that she then called in the strength of a wrestler named Narcissus, who strangled the wretched man (192 A.D).

Could the purple be degraded to a lower depth? Before six months had expired, after Pertinax, once a poor charcoal-burner, had been raised to the throne by the Prætorians, only to be pierced soon by a Prætorian's lance, the imperial power was *sold by auction* for a sum which allowed each of the guards thirty sesterces. Long before **193** the year had reached its end, Didius Julianus, A.D. the purchaser, who always walked abroad under a storm of hisses and cursing, died under the axe of the common headsman.

As we look down the long list of Emperors, who reigned in Rome from Commodus to Augustulus, we see a few—and but a few—worthy of notice and respect. When we have selected Septimius Severus, Aurelian, Diocletian, Constantine the Great, Julian the Apostate, and Theodosius, the rest may, without loss to history, be swept from the page.

SEPTIMIUS SEVERUS, a general of Germany, was declared Emperor by the Senate upon the death of Didius Julianus. He had two rivals for the empire—Niger in Syria, and Albinus in Britain. The defeat of the one at Issus and of the other at Lyons left him master of the field. A successful war against the Parthians also raised his name as a soldier. But his expedition into Britain forms the most notable episode of his reign.

Passing into Britain in 208 A.D., he pushed his way northward by the Roman *streets* of paved stone, so long as these afforded him footing; and he then committed his army and himself to the wild Caledonian forests. Most harassing attacks of the woodmen troubled the march. Out from the forest glades would rush a horde of savages, brandishing dirks, and shaking with horrid noise the brazen rattles that tipped the handles of their spears. The hungry Roman soldiers would sometimes find a sheep or an ox straying near the path, and when they ran to seize the prize, would find claymores whirling round their devoted heads. Through all these perils Severus forced his way to the promontory between the Cromarty and Moray Friths. The Romans, except for the name of conquest, had decidedly the worst of the war. Severus died at York in 211 A.D.

AURELIAN, whose father was a husbandman, raised himself by valour and strictness of discipline to the highest military command. In 270 A.D. the Legions of the Danube claimed the imperial purple for him. He conquered the Germans and the Vandals; but the chief interest of his reign centres in his war with Zenobia, the celebrated Queen of Palmyra.

This lady, the widow of Odenathus, held her warlike court at Palmyra, a strong and beautiful city in the heart of the Syrian Desert, where amid palm-trees crumbling pillars of colossal size still attest its ancient greatness. Bright black eyes, pearly teeth, a frank and pleasant manner, ability to talk in Greek and in Egyptian, as well as in her native Syriac, helped to account for her influence over the men she ruled. She rode on horseback with a helmet on, and wore a skirt whose purple border clanked with pendent jewels. Proceeding by way of the Hellespont into Syria, Aurelian met and defeated the army of Zenobia at Emesa. He then besieged Palmyra, which the Queen defended fiercely with balistæ and engines that flung fire. She counted on aid from Persia, and on
273 A.D. the lack of food in the desert; but both hopes failed. While trying to escape, she was seized.

The city, treated mildly at first, was afterwards given up to massacre and pillage as a punishment for revolt. The stately Queen, after decorating the Triumph of Aurelian, retired to an estate near Rome, where she lived in rural quiet. Among those slain at Palmyra was Longinus, Greek tutor to the Queen, and author of a treatise *On the Sublime*.

Aurelian was murdered by conspirators in 275 A.D.

DIOCLETIAN was raised to the throne by the soldiers,

when the dead body of Numerian, slain many days before, was found in the litter, whose seclusion he had sought owing to inflammation of the eyes. Diocletian ran his sword through Aper the murderer, crying out, "See, I have killed a boar." It had been foretold that to kill a boar would win for him a throne: and thus he fulfilled the prophecy, 284 A.D.

His reign is remarkable for the division of the empire—first into two parts, when he appointed Maximian, originally a slave like himself, to share his power—and later, 292 A.D., when each Augustus chose a Cæsar to assist him. Diocletian, whose centre of government was Nicomedia, chose Galerius, once a herdsman; Maximian, ruling chiefly from Milan, took Constantius Chlorus (the Sallow). Diocletian, keeping Asia and Egypt, assigned Thrace and Illyria to his Cæsar; while Maximian, holding Italy and Africa, sent Constantius to Gaul and Spain.

Besides these important changes in the Government, we have to note in this reign the insurrection of Carausius in Britain, and the infliction of the last and worst of the persecutions that fell upon the Christians under the old Roman Empire.

Carausius, the Menapian, was captain of the Channel Fleet in the British seas, when an order came from Rome to put him to death, because he was suspected of enriching himself by piratical incursions. He defied the edict, took to his ships, and seized Gessoriacum, which we call *Boulogne*. He ruled in Britain for seven years, until one of his officers named Allectus murdered him, 297 A.D. Allectus held sway for three years longer: but the island was then recovered for Diocletian by Constantius Chlorus.

In the year 303 the most terrible of the persecutions, to which the Christians were subjected, broke out in Nicomedia, a city of Bithynia. The church was razed to the ground, and all copies of the Bible found were burned. Galerius, the son-in-law of the Emperor, was the author of these deeds, and of the dreadful edict of persecution that commanded Christians to be degraded in every part of the empire. A man who tore down the placard was roasted to death; and from the Alps to Armenia the fires of death began to burn.

303 A.D.

The persecution was still raging, when in 305 A.D. Diocletian abdicated his imperial throne, obliging Maximian to do the same at Milan; nor did it spend its violence until 311, when Galerius, smitten with fear of coming death, published an edict favourable to the Christians.

In the year 308 A.D. no fewer than *six* Emperors divided among themselves the Roman world. Sixteen years of warfare removed all but one, CONSTANTINE THE GREAT, who took to himself the dominion of those he had overcome. From 324 to 337 he continued to be Emperor of Rome. He is commonly regarded as the first of the Christian Emperors; and a strange story is told of a Fiery Cross, which he saw hung in the sky, with the motto below it, "In this conquer," while he was preparing to contest the empire with his colleague Maxentius at Saxa Rubra near Rome. But his tenderness to the Christians, exhibited chiefly in the famous edict of toleration passed at Milan in 313 A.D., seems to have been rather a matter of policy than of conviction.

324 A.D.

The chief event of Constantine's reign was the adoption as a new capital of that city on the Bosporus, which still bears this Emperor's name. The position is one of striking importance, for a city built upon that narrow strait commands at once Europe and Asia, and controls the communication between the Black Sea and the Mediterranean. The name New Rome was given at first to the beautiful city of gold and marble, which Constantine made out of old Byzantium.

Constantine adopted a new policy as well as a new capital. He vastly increased the titles of nobility and invented swelling Asiatic names of grandeur. He gave to the Curials the task of collecting the new and heavy direct taxes laid upon the people. And, breaking up the famous Legions into small bands, he placed the army, now separate from the civil service, under eight Masters-General.

The death of Constantine in 337 A.D., left the purple to be rent and stained by the conflicts of his three sons.

JULIAN THE APOSTATE derived his historical name from his renunciation of Christianity, which took place about 351 A.D., ten years before his accession to the throne. He reigned for only two years (361-363), during which he tried by writing, by building pagan fanes, by an attempted restoration of the Jewish Temple (in order to disprove prophecy), by every means his philosophic mind could devise, to force the Roman people to return to their old gods. But all was in vain. He was slain by an arrow-wound in the side, received while he was in the East, warring with the Persians.

The distinct division of the Roman Empire into West and East dates from the reign of Valentinian and Valens 364 A.D.

THEODOSIUS became Emperor of the East in 379 A.D. Three years earlier, by permission of Valens, a host of Goths, fleeing before the savage Huns, had established themselves to the number of a million to the south of the Danube, a great natural frontier of the Roman Empire. Against their incursions Theodosius directed all his energies. He dealt rigorously with Paganism, and endeavoured to root out various heresies from the Christian Church. He died at Milan in 395 A.D.

About eighty years now completed the fall of Rome. Honorius, the unworthy son of Theodosius, fled to Ravenna before the approach of Alaric the Visigoth, who seized and plundered Rome in 410. Genseric overswept Africa with his Vandals, while Attila the Hun soon afterwards invaded Gaul. The last dying flicker of old Roman greatness was displayed on the field of Chalons, where Aëtius and Theodoric turned the flood of savagery back by a decisive defeat (451 A.D.). The Huns then moved southward, and crossed the Alps into Italy. Attila threatened Rome, but the intercession of Bishop Leo saved the capital for a time. This prelate was less successful in his attempt to avert the attack of the Vandals in 455 A.D. For a fortnight these destroyers ran riot through the Forum and its surrounding streets.

Ricimer, a soldier of fortune, who made and unmade Emperors, was master of the Eternal City for many years of her latest existence. And with Romulus Augustulus, who at Ravenna made abject submission to Odoacer, a Gothic chieftain of the tribe Heruli, the long line of Roman Emperors came to an end in 476 A.D. The Eastern or Byzantine Empire, as it came to be called, survived for all but a thousand years, and then yielded to the Ottomans only after a series of fierce attacks, which, spreading over a century, culminated in the great siege of Constantinople, 1453 A.D.

LATER LATIN WRITERS.

GELLIUS, born probably at Rome—lived between 117 A.D. and 180 A.D.—author of *Noctes Atticæ*, a miscellany, written during the winter nights in a country house near Athens.

APPULEIUS, native of Madura in Africa—educated at Carthage and Athens—lived during the second century A.D.—author of a satirical romance called *The Golden Ass*, and other works.

CURTIUS, historian—ascribed by Niebuhr to the age of Septimius Severus, but this is mere conjecture—author of a *History of Alexander the Great.*

ULPIAN, great Latin jurist—of a family originally from Tyre—time of birth unknown—wrote in reign of Caracalla (211-217)—chief adviser of Alexander Severus—slain by soldiers in the palace 228 A.D. —chief work *Ad Edictum*, very largely used in compiling Justinian's *Digest.*

EUTROPIUS, historian—flourished under Constantine the Great and Julian the Apostate—author of a *Compendium of Roman History,* to the accession of Valens.

AMMIANUS, historian—native of Syrian Antioch—flourished between 350 A.D. and 390 A.D.—author of a *Roman History*, from Nerva to Valens, inclusive.

CLAUDIAN, last of the Latin classic poets—lived under Theodosius and his sons—native of Alexandria—chief works his *Panegyrics*— author also of an unfinished epic, *The Rape of Proserpine.*

ROMAN CHRONOLOGY.

THE MONARCHY.

	B.C.
Building of Rome—Accession of Romulus,	753
Accession of Numa,	715
Accession of Tullus Hostilius,	672
Accession of Ancus Marcius,	640
Accession of Tarquin the Elder,	616
Accession of Servius Tullius,	578
Accession of Tarquin the Haughty,	534
Expulsion of the Tarquins, and establishment of the Republic,	509

FIFTH CENTURY, B.C.
THE REPUBLIC.

Lartius appointed the first Dictator,	499
Battle of Lake Regillus,	496
First Secession of the Plebs,	494
Tribunes of the Plebs first appointed,	493
Coriolanus threatens Rome,	491
Spurius Cassius proposes an Agrarian Law,	486
Cincinnatus defeats the Æquians,	458
Decemvirs chosen to frame a new Code of Laws,	451
The Twelve Tables set up,	450
Virginius kills his daughter—Second Secession to Mons Sacer,	449
The Canuleian Law passed,	445
Military Tribunes appointed with consular power,	—

FOURTH CENTURY, B.C.

Ten years' siege of Veii closed,	396
Gauls victorious at the Alia,	390
Sack of Rome,	—
The Licinian Rogations passed,	367
Sextius the first Plebeian Consul,	366

THE SAMNITE WARS.

	B.C.
First Samnite War,	343–341
The Final Latin War,	340–338
Second Samnite War,	326–304
Disgrace of the Romans at Caudine Forks,	321
Ogulnian Law, admitting Plebeians to the priesthood,	300

THIRD CENTURY, B.C.

THE SAMNITE WARS CONTINUED.

Third Samnite War,	299–290
Roman victory at Sentinum over the Samnites and the Gauls,	295
Submission of Samnium,	290
Gauls defeated at Lake Vadimo,	283

EXPEDITION OF PYRRHUS.

Landing of Pyrrhus in Italy,	281
Defeat of the Romans at Heraclea,	280
Defeat of the Romans also at Asculum,	279
Pyrrhus defeated at Beneventum,	275

Rome, finally defeating the Samnites, is left mistress of Southern Italy,	268
Rome aids the Mamertines in Messana,	264

THE FIRST PUNIC WAR.

The First Punic War,	263–241
Siege of Agrigentum,	262
Duilius defeats a Punic fleet at Mylæ,	260
Another Punic fleet defeated at Ecnomus,	256
Defeat and capture of Regulus at Tunis,	255
Carthaginians defeated at Panormus,	250
The Romans besiege Lilybæum,	249
Roman victory at Ægusa,	241

Gauls defeated at Telamon,	225
Hannibal elected to the command in Spain,	220
Siege of Saguntum,	219

SECOND PUNIC WAR.

Second or Great Punic War,	218–202
Hannibal begins his march,	May, 218

ROMAN CHRONOLOGY. 143

	B.C.
Hannibal reaches Italy,	Sept., 218
Skirmish on the Ticinus,	Dec., —
Battle of the Trebia,	Dec., —
Battle of Lake Trasimene,	... 217
Battle of Cannæ,	Aug. 2, 216
Hannibal's first reverse (at Nola),	—
First Macedonian War,	215–205
Siege of Capua,	214–211
Siege of Syracuse by Marcellus,	214–212
Publius Scipio elected Proconsul for Spain,	211
Capture of New Carthage,	209
Battle of Bæcula,	208
Battle of the Metaurus,	207
Spain a Roman province,	206
P. Scipio lands in Africa,	204
Battle of Zama,	202
Peace with Carthage,	201
Second Macedonian War,	200–197

SECOND CENTURY, B.C.

Battle of Cynoscephalæ—Philip of Macedon defeated,	197
The Syrian War,	192–190
Battle of Magnesia,	190
Cato elected to the Censorship,	184
Death of Hannibal and of Scipio Africanus,	183
Treaty of Gracchus pacifies Spain,	179
Third Macedonian War,	171–168
Battle of Pydna,	168
THIRD PUNIC WAR,	149–146
Fall of Carthage and of Corinth—Greece and Libya become Roman provinces,	146
Assassination of Viriathus the Lusitanian,	140
Numantia taken by Scipio Minor,	133
First Slave War,	133–131
Tribuneship and death of Tiberius Gracchus,	133
Supposed murder of Scipio Minor,	129
Caius Gracchus made Tribune,	123
Death of Caius Gracchus,	121
Jugurthine War,	111–105
Marius first elected Consul,	107
Second Slave War in Sicily,	103–101
Teutones defeated at Aquæ Sextiæ (Aix),	102
Cimbri defeated on the Raudine Plain,	101

FIRST CENTURY, B.C.

	B.C.
Sedition and death of Saturninus,	100
Attempted reform and murder of Drusus,	91
The Social or Marsic War,	90–88
First Mithridatic War,	88–84
Flight of Marius to Africa,	88
Rome occupied by Marius—dreadful massacre,	87
Death of Marius,	86
Athens taken and burned by Sulla,	—
Landing of Sulla in Italy,	83
Second Mithridatic War,	83–81
Battle at the Colline Gate of Rome,	82
Proscriptions of Sulla deluge Rome with blood,	—
Sulla lays down the Dictatorship,	80
His death at Puteoli,	78
Third Mithridatic War,	74–63
Sertorius murdered in Spain,	72
The Gladiatorial War of Spartacus,	73–71

POMPEY AND CÆSAR.

Consulship of Pompey and Crassus,	70
Pompey clears the Mediterranean of pirates,	67
Supersedes Lucullus in Mithridatic War,	66
Suicide of Mithridates in the Crimea,	63
The conspiracy of Catiline,	—
Julius Cæsar made Consul—First Triumvirate,	59
Banishment of Cicero,	58
Cæsar sets out for Gaul,	—
Partition of the provinces among the Triumvirs,	55
Cæsar's first invasion of Britain,	—
Defeat and death of Crassus in Parthia,	53
Cæsar conquers Vercingetorix in Gaul,	52
Cæsar crosses the Rubicon,	49
Battle of Pharsalia—Death of Pompey,	48
Pompeians in Africa defeated at Thapsus—Suicide of Cato,	46
Pompeians in Spain defeated at Munda,	45
Murder of Cæsar,	15th March, 44

Antony defeated at Mutina,	43
The Second Triumvirate—Antony, Octavian, and Lepidus—Death of Cicero,	—
Defeat and death of Brutus and Cassius at Philippi,	42
Naval war with Sextus Pompey,	38–36

ROMAN CHRONOLOGY.

	B.C.
Battle of Actium,	31
Death of Antony and Cleopatra,	30
Octavian called Augustus and Imperator,	27
BIRTH OF JESUS CHRIST,	3

FIRST CENTURY OF THE CHRISTIAN ERA.

	A.D.
Army of Varus destroyed in Germany,	9
Death of Augustus,	14
Reign of Tiberius,	14–37
Germanicus defeats Arminius,	16
Death of Germanicus in Syria,	19
Prætorians collected at Rome,	23
Retirement of Tiberius to Capreæ,	26
Death of Sejanus,	31
Murder of Tiberius,	37
Reign of Caligula,	37–41
Reign of Claudius,	41–54
Invasion of Britain,	43
Caractacus made prisoner,	51
Claudius poisoned,	54
Reign of Nero,	54–68
Defeat and death of Boadicea in Britain,	61
Great fire at Rome—First Christian persecution,	64
Nero's death,	68
Galba murdered,	69
Otho kills himself,	—
Vitellius murdered,	—
Reign of Vespasian,	69–79
Destruction of Jerusalem,	70
Julius Agricola Proprætor of Britain,	78
Reign of Titus,	79–81
Great eruption of Vesuvius,	79
Reign of Domitian,	81–96
Agricola's victory at the Grampians,	84
Reign of Nerva,	96–98
Reign of Trajan,	98–117

SECOND CENTURY, A.D.

Final conquest of Dacia,	104
Reign of Hadrian,	117–138
Erects a wall in Britain,	120
Publishes *Edictum Perpetuum*,	131
Reign of Antoninus Pius,	138–161

	A.D.
Reign of Aurelius,	161–180
Victory over the Quadi,	174
Reign of Commodus,	180–192
Prætorians sell the purple by auction,	193
Reign of Septimius Severus,	193–211

THIRD CENTURY, A.D.

Expedition of Severus to Britain,	208
Death of Severus at York,	211
Reign of Aurelian,	270–275
Siege of Palmyra—Capture of Zenobia,	273
Reign of Diocletian—He divides the empire with Maximian,	284–305
Carausius assumes the purple in Britain,	289
Fourfold division of the Roman Empire,	292
Assassination of Carausius,	297

FOURTH CENTURY, A.D.

Christians persecuted by Diocletian and Galerius	303–311
Empire divided among *six*,	308
Edict of Toleration by Constantine,	313
Reign of Constantine,	324–337
Constantinople selected as a Capital,	330
Reign of Julian the Apostate,	361–363
Division of the empire by Valentinian and Valens,	364
Reign of Theodosius,	379–395

FIFTH CENTURY, A.D.

Alaric the Visigoth sacks Rome,	410
Genseric the Vandal takes Carthage,	439
Attila the Hun defeated at Chalons,	451
The Vandals pillage Rome,	455
Reign of Majorian,	457–461
Augustulus submits to Odoacer—Fall of the Western Empire,	476

NELSON'S SCHOOL SERIES.

ENGLISH READING-BOOKS,

ADAPTED TO THE

STANDARDS OF THE REVISED CODE.

"A more interesting set of Reading-Books we have never seen. We are not surprised by their great popularity and extensive sale. . . . We have had the advantage of examining with care the entire Series, and we cannot too strongly express the sense we entertain of the taste and judgment the books display, or of their great educational value."—*The Rev. Dr. Hall, (in the Evangelical Witness,) Commissioner of National Education, Ireland.*

THE SERIES IS NOW COMPLETE AS FOLLOWS:—

STANDARD I.

1. **STEP BY STEP;** or, The Child's First Lesson-Book. 18mo. Parts I. and II. Price 2d. each.
2. **SEQUEL TO "STEP BY STEP."** 18mo. Price 4d.

STANDARD II.

3. **THE YOUNG READER**—New No. 3. Beautifully Illustrated. Price 6d.

Previously published for this stage, and still to be had.

No. 3 READING-BOOK. Price 6d.
THE FOUR SEASONS. Price 6d.

STANDARDS III. & IV.

4. **NEW FOURTH BOOK.** Beautifully Illustrated. Price 10d.; or with Book Slate, 1s.

"Out of sight the best Elementary Reading-book we have seen."—*Museum and English Journal of Education.*

STANDARD IV.

5. **JUNIOR READER.** No. I. Post 8vo, cloth. Price 1s. 3d.

STANDARD V.

6. **JUNIOR READER.** No. II. Post 8vo, cloth. Price 1s. 6d.

STANDARD VI.

7. **THE SENIOR READER.** Post 8vo, cloth. Price 2s. 6d.
8. **THE ADVANCED READER.** Post 8vo. 400 pages. Price 2s. 6d.

"We have no hesitation in pronouncing this the best 'Advanced Reader' that we know. . . . The book is one of deep interest from beginning to end, and will be read by the teacher as well as the pupil with growing pleasure."
—*The Museum and English Journal of Education, Dec.* 1865.

NELSON'S SCHOOL SERIES.

ENGLISH READING-BOOKS.
EXTRA VOLUMES.

NEW CLASS-BOOK OF ENGLISH POETRY. PART I.—JUNIOR DIVISION. Small Type Edition, price 6d. Large Type Edition, price 1s.
    PART II.—SENIOR DIVISION. Small Type Edition, price 6d. Large Type Edition, price 1s.
    THE TWO PARTS BOUND IN ONE. Small Type Edition, price 1s. Large Type Edition, price 2s.

THE CHEMISTRY OF COMMON THINGS. By STEVENSON MACADAM, F.R.S.E., F.C.S. With upwards of Sixty Diagrams. 12mo, price 1s. 6d.

    CONTENTS:—The Atmosphere, and its Relations to Plants and Animals.—The Plant, and what it Feeds on.—The Plant, and what it Yields us.—The Animal, and what it Feeds on.—The Earth, or Soil, in its Relations to Plants and Animals.—The Decay of Plants and Animals.—The Circulation of Matter, &c., &c.

READINGS FROM THE BEST AUTHORS. Edited by A. H. BRYCE, LL.D. 12mo, cloth. Price 1s. 6d.

READINGS FROM THE BEST AUTHORS. Second Book. Edited by A. H. BRYCE, LL.D. Post 8vo, cloth. Price 2s.

MILTON'S PARADISE LOST AND PARADISE REGAINED. With Notes for the Use of Schools. By the Rev. J. EDMONDSTON. 12mo, cloth. Price 2s. 6d.

CLASS-BOOK OF ENGLISH LITERATURE; with Biographical Sketches, Critical Notices, and Illustrative Extracts. For the use of Schools and Students. By ROBERT ARMSTRONG, English Master, Madras College, St. Andrews; and THOMAS ARMSTRONG, Edinburgh; Authors of "English Composition" and "English Etymology." Post 8vo. Price 3s.

THE ENGLISH WORD-BOOK: A Manual Exhibiting the Sources, Structure, and Affinities of English Words. By JOHN GRAHAM. Price 1s.
    Also kept in Two Parts.
    PART I.—PREFIXES AND POSTFIXES. Price 3d.
    PART II.—ROOTS, DERIVATIVES, AND MEANINGS. Price 6d.

WORD EXPOSITOR AND SPELLING GUIDE: A School Manual Exhibiting the Spelling, Pronunciation, Meaning, and Derivation of all the Important and Peculiar Words in the English Language. With Copious Exercises for Examination and Dictation. By GEORGE COUTIE, A.M. 12mo, cloth. Price 1s. 3d.

NELSON'S SCHOOL SERIES.

SCHOOL HISTORIES.

BY W. F. COLLIER, LL.D.

ENGLISH HISTORY for Junior Classes. 12mo, cloth. Price 1s. 6d.

HISTORY OF THE BRITISH EMPIRE. With Tables of the Leading Events of each Period—Lists of Contemporary Sovereigns—Dates of Battles—Chapters on the Social Changes of each Period, &c. 12mo, cloth. Price 2s.

"Dr. Collier's book is unrivalled as a School History of the British Empire. The arrangement is admirable."—*English Journal of Education.*

THE GREAT EVENTS OF HISTORY, from the Beginning of the Christian Era till the Present Time. 12mo, cloth. Price 2s. 6d.

HISTORY OF ENGLISH LITERATURE. In a Series of Biographical Sketches. 12mo, cloth. Price 3s. 6d.

BY THE REV. J. MACKENZIE.

HISTORY OF SCOTLAND. 12mo, cloth. Price 1s. 6d.

BY THE REV. R. HUNTER.

HISTORY OF INDIA, from the Earliest Ages to the Fall of the East India Company, and the Proclamation of Queen Victoria in 1858. 282 pages, with Woodcuts. Foolscap 8vo, cloth. Price 1s. 6d.

BY THE REV. DR. BLAIKIE.

BIBLE HISTORY, in connection with the General History of the World. With Descriptions of Scripture Localities. 470 pages 12mo, with Maps. Price 3s.

This volume has been prepared mainly with a view to the instruction of Schools and Families. Its plan differs in many respects from that of any other Bible History.

1. It follows the great outline of the Bible Narrative,—arranging and classifying the leading facts, *so as to aid eye and memory in grasping the whole.*

2. For *vivifying the Narrative*, it takes advantage of the mass of Biblical Illustration supplied in Recent Researches, Travels, Expeditions, &c.

3. It describes briefly the *chief Countries, Towns, and other scenes of Bible History,* as they occur.

4. It glances at the *History and Progress of the Leading Nations of the World,*—showing what was going on elsewhere while the History of the Bible was being enacted.

QUESTIONS ON BLAIKIE'S BIBLE HISTORY. Price 6d.

NELSON'S SCHOOL SERIES.

GEOGRAPHIES, ATLASES, &c.

GEOGRAPHIES.

ELEMENTARY GEOGRAPHY. By Thomas G. Dick. Post 8vo, cloth. Price 1s.

NEW CLASS-BOOK OF GEOGRAPHY, Physical and Political. By Robert Anderson, Head Master, Normal Institution, Edinburgh. 12mo, cloth. Price 1s. 9d.

MODERN GEOGRAPHY, for the Use of Schools. By Robert Anderson. Foolscap 8vo, cloth. Price 1s. 6d.

EXERCISES IN GEOGRAPHY, adapted to Anderson's Geography. 18mo, cloth. Price 6d.

GEOGRAPHY FOR JUNIOR CLASSES. By Robert Anderson. 18mo, cloth. Price 11d.

BIBLE GEOGRAPHY. By the Rev. W. G. Blaikie, D.D. With Coloured Maps, Price 1s. 12mo, cloth. Or with the Maps mounted on Cloth, 1s. 3d.

ATLASES.

With Divisions and Measurements in English Miles.

NELSON'S SENIOR ATLAS. Containing 23 Large Quarto Maps, full coloured. Reduced copies of Nelson's Wall Maps. In boards. Price 3s. 6d.

NELSON'S JUNIOR ATLAS. Containing 9 Quarto Maps. Full coloured. Stiff cover. Price 1s. 6d.

NELSON'S SHILLING ATLAS. Containing 16 Maps, plain. Stiff wrapper, 4to.

ARITHMETICS.

THE FIRST BOOK OF ARITHMETIC. 12mo. Price 6d.

THE SECOND BOOK OF ARITHMETIC. Part I. By W. Stanyer. 12mo, cloth. Price 1s. 6d. With "Answers to the Exercises." Price 1s. 9d.

EXERCISES IN MENTAL AND SLATE ARITHMETIC FOR BEGINNERS. By J. Copland. 18mo, cloth. Price 4d.

www.ingramcontent.com/pod-product-compliance
Lightning Source LLC
Chambersburg PA
CBHW030309170426
43202CB00009B/926